OMG!

WEDDING STORIES

By Alex & Elizabeth Lluch

from WedSpace.com

WS Publishing Group
San Diego, California 92119

OMG! Wedding Stories
From WedSpace.com

By Alex & Elizabeth Lluch
Published by WS Publishing Group
San Diego, California 92119
© Copyright 2010 by WS Publishing Group

Design by:
David Defenbaugh, Sarah Jang; WS Publishing Group

Image Credits:
Cover photo, bride © Jason Lugo/iStockphoto
Cover photo, groom © Oleksandr Gumerov/iStockphoto

For more information on this and many other best-selling
books visit www.WSPublishingGroup.com.
E-mail: info@WSPublishingGroup.com

ISBN 13: 978-1-934386-97-2

Printed in China

Contents

Contents

Contents

Introduction

Weddings are beautiful, memorable and special for everyone involved. However, with so many details, guests, and vendors coming together, something is bound to go awry on the Big Day. Between bungled proposals, nightmare weather, crazy in-laws, vendor mishaps, and regular old Murphy's Law, it seems that no wedding is ever quite perfect.

For *OMG! Wedding Stories* we compiled the most hilarious, outrageous, embarrassing, and inspiring true wedding tales from members of WedSpace.com, the top social networking site for engaged couples to connect with other brides, guests, and local vendors.

We believe this book will help engaged couples laugh, relax and stay realistic as they plan their weddings. After reading this book you'll realize, no matter what goes wrong on your wedding day, it probably won't compare to these crazy tales!

From the engagement to planning the wedding to the Big Day to the honeymoon, these stories will have married couples, engaged couples, wedding pros and anyone who has ever been a wedding guest laughing, gasping in shock, and thinking, "Thank goodness that wasn't me!"

OMG! Wedding Stories reminds you that no wedding is perfect, and the least you can do is laugh about it and cherish the memories.

We would love to include your crazy, funny or outrageous wedding story in our next printing! If you have an engagement, wedding or honeymoon story you would like to submit for a future edition of this or one of our other top-selling wedding planning books, please email info@ WSPublishingGroup.com and put "OMG Wedding Stories" in the subject line. Or, write to us at WS Publishing Group, 7290 Navajo Road, Suite 207; San Diego, California 92119.

We love to hear from brides and grooms like you — that's why WS Publishing Group has become the best-selling publisher of wedding planning books!

Sincerely,

Elizabeth H. Lluch

Proposal

Indecent Exposure

- Jaimie Dobson

My boyfriend Dan and I had been having a long-distance relationship after college — he lived in D.C. and I was living in Nashville. For the Thanksgiving holiday, Dan was coming to stay with my family and me, and I was very, very excited to get to spend 5 days with him. The night before Thanksgiving, Dan said he wanted to take me out to a nice dinner, so I got dressed up in a cute dress, tights and boots and we went to one of my favorite restaurants in the Hillsboro area.

As we were driving to dinner, it started to snow! We got a nice table by the big windows of the restaurant, Dan ordered a bottle of wine, and it was just a perfect, romantic night, watching the snow and enjoying being together. Dan seemed almost giddy; I should have realized why, but I didn't. I was just loving the night.

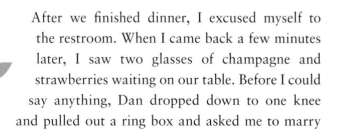

After we finished dinner, I excused myself to the restroom. When I came back a few minutes later, I saw two glasses of champagne and strawberries waiting on our table. Before I could say anything, Dan dropped down to one knee and pulled out a ring box and asked me to marry him! I literally squealed, then started crying and hugging him and saying, "Yes, yes, yes" over and over again. I was completely surprised and completely ecstatic.

Right as I was hugging him, a lady from a nearby table came over and tapped me on the shoulder. Assuming she was congratulating me on my engagement, I gave her a big hug and said, "Thank you." She looked puzzled and leaned in to whisper to me, "No, honey, your dress is tucked into your tights. Your panties are showing."

I think I froze. I reached back and, sure enough, I'd tucked the back of my dress into my tights by accident while coming out of the restroom. I fixed my dress and sat down as quickly as I could. Dan was confused as to why my happy face turned bright red just then, but he joined me at the table to toast with our champagne. It was a strange feeling — the happiest moment of my life, but I also felt like crawling into a hole!

So, an entire restaurant — couples on dates, families with kids, waiters, everyone — saw my underwear while my boyfriend proposed to me. I'll get over it, and Dan and I are looking forward to getting married this summer. Still, I'm sure that's a sight the people in that restaurant won't soon forget, although I'd like to!

Beach Blunder

- Jason and Julia Wang

When I realized I wanted to marry Julia, I wanted that day to come as soon as possible. So I saved up money and shopped at many different stores looking for a ring that would be perfect for this occasion.

I knew I needed a proposal plan. I chose to go with an intimate setting where it would be just the two of us. Julia likes to do outdoor activities, so I decided we would go fishing and swimming at Joe Pool Lake, the perfect destination for our engagement.

Julia works a lot — one of my favorite qualities is that she is a very hard worker. She is a full-time student, putting in 32 to 40 hours a week at work, and volunteers at church. So when she said, "I have the afternoon off tomorrow," I was really happy. I thought to myself, *This is perfect!*

The next day, we drove to Joe Pool Lake, got to the dock, bought our fishing gear, and went out to the fishing area. I had purchased a fishing tackle box and put letters spelling out "Will You Marry Me" in the container. Unfortunately, the fishing area was hot, steamy, rusty … basically, disgusting.

There were also a lot of other people. This was not what I expected the proposal setting to be like. I thought, *I am not going to propose in this dump. Perhaps, the beach will be better.* I asked Julia if she didn't mind ditching the fishing idea and just go swimming. She gladly accepted.

So, we drove to the beach. The water was rather cold, but I jumped in regardless. I swam as far as I could until I got tired. Finally, I got out of the lake and went to where Julia was sitting. I got everything ready. The camera was set. The container with the words "Will You Marry Me" was in one hand. The ring was in my camera bag. I went up to Julia and said, "I'm sorry fishing wasn't that fun, but I bought you something from the fishing store." When she saw the words, she smiled, and I was so happy. Then, I reached for the ring box in my camera bag. I opened it, and guess what? No ring. The ring had fallen out onto the shore and the waves had washed it away!

> I reached for the ring box in my camera bag, opened it, and guess what? ...

We spent two hours looking for the ring. We prayed and asked God for a miracle. Finally, we decided to stop. I told Julia that I very much wanted to marry her even though I dropped the ring. She said she wanted to marry me as well. I still wanted to officially propose — get down on one knee, ask her to marry me, and slip a ring on her finger. I remembered Julia had a ring in her jewelry box that looked similar to the one that I had purchased. I asked her if I could have that ring. We thanked God for the day and went home where I got down on one knee and said, "Will you marry me?" She said yes, and I slipped on the ring.

We were engaged, yet both of us were still filled with tears. I went to my house, uploaded some pictures of the day on Flickr and changed my Facebook status. The cheers from family and friends started rolling in. It was great to see so many friends excited for Julia and me, but I was still sad that I had lost the ring. In the midst of the sadness, there were messages of encouragement from Julia's family. They encouraged me to go back out again the next day and look for the ring. I assured them, "I will go tomorrow morning."

I still wanted to officially propose — get down on one knee, ask her to marry me, and slip a ring on her finger.

My soul was torn because I was so happy, but I had never seen Julia so hurt before in our two-and-half-year relationship. I was sad that I had contributed to her sadness. I prayed for peace for us both. Around 10:30 p.m. I talked to Julia. She said she was coming to terms with the lost ring. We both felt much better and said our goodnights.

I very much wanted to keep my promise to Julia's family, so I woke up early, rented a metal detector, and drove back to Joe Pool Lake and started searching. My thoughts and prayers were on Julia. I kept looking and searching. Suddenly, an hour later, where the water and shore meet,

I saw a silver circle sticking up out of the sand. I got down on all fours and picked it up. It was the ring!

I got home and emailed Julia's family the great news. Then I told Julia to meet me for lunch. She asked if I had found the ring. I said, "No, but I'll see you for lunch." Just a little white lie, but I wanted to see her face when I surprised her.

At lunch, we hugged and sat in silence for a few seconds. Then, I said, "Well, I'm sorry about everything that happened yesterday, but I got you something." I gave her the box and the ring was inside. She quickly took off her old ring and put on the real one. We thanked God that everything worked out. After that stressful proposal gone wrong, we're just so excited to be getting married!

Not-So-Perfect Proposal

- Eris Young

It was a year ago, on my birthday. My boyfriend, Brad, was working as the chef for an exclusive restaurant at Caesars Palace in Las Vegas. We went there for dinner where he had reserved one of the best tables in the house. When we arrived at the restaurant, a bottle  of Perrier Jouet was chilling on the table and a single white rose lay across my plate. Our waiter efficiently opened the bottle, dropped a bright red raspberry into each of our glasses, and poured.

While I was perfectly happy enjoying my champagne and people-watching, Brad kept insisting that he was starving and that I "drink up" so we could order appetizers. I hurriedly swallowed the rest of my drink and, to my horror, began to choke on my raspberry. A nearby staff member immediately noticed my predicament. He rushed over, stood me up in front of God, Brad and what seemed like the entire universe, wrapped his arms around me and began performing the Heimlich maneuver!

Almost immediately, the article that was lodged in my throat projected out of my mouth and landed directly in the bread basket at the center of the table, right on top of a lovely slice of raisin pumpernickel bread.

Gratitude and relief were brief as I looked into the bread basket and discovered that I had not been choking on just a raspberry but rather an engagement ring surrounding a raspberry! Brad, who I am quite sure did not expect this turn of events, didn't miss a beat. He picked up the ring, dipped it into his water glass and wiped it clean, and then dropped to one knee.

He gently asked me if I would do him the honor of becoming his wife. Amidst a flutter of emotions and a captive audience of restaurant customers, I managed to utter a soft-spoken, "Yes." The restaurant customers and employees who had been enjoying the evening's performance began to applaud. We opted not to have dinner after all that had transpired and decided to head home. I decided to use the ladies room before we left.

I was mortified! I just wanted to crawl under the nearest table and die.

At this particular restaurant, the restrooms are located at the top of a curved staircase. I climbed the stairs and, after a proper amount of primping, emerged from the ladies room and began to make my descent back to ground level. I saw Brad waiting for me at the bottom of the stairs, smiling. I glanced at my finger to admire my shiny new engagement ring. I guess that's when it happened. As I was looking at my ring, I wasn't looking at the step in front of me. As such, I missed the step and began plummeting toward my certain death. And with every step I rode downward, my dress inched upward, until both of us came to a stop; me at the bottom of the staircase, my dress at the top of my waist, thus exposing the Spanx Higher Power foundation garment I was wearing.

I was mortified! I just wanted to crawl under the nearest table and die. But Brad, who witnessed the entire spectacle, did not run, hide, ignore or attempt to avoid the situation in any way. Instead, he helped me to my feet and with the most sincere look on his face, whispered to me, "I'm going to love being married to you."

Pawn Shop Proposal

- Ruth Thaler-Carter

My now-husband and I had been together about three months when we went to a neighborhood pawn shop to buy him a new watch. He started asking me what I thought of various diamond rings on display. I was entranced by a ring with a beautiful pink tourmaline in a gold setting. Not paying much attention to the reason for his question, I also said I liked one that had six diamonds around a central one. We got him his watch and left the shop.

Out on the sidewalk, he stopped and said, "I'd like to give you that ring." I said something like, "Oh, I loved that ring — it's so me!" and he repeated, "I'd like to give you that diamond ring that you liked." Silly me, I said, "What do you mean?" and he asked, "Will you marry me?"

I was totally flabbergasted. We had known each other only three months and had been inseparable almost from day one, but I wasn't expecting a proposal. All I could do was grab him for a big kiss.

Before I could manage to say "Yes," we heard

someone yell, "Hey, enough with the public display of affection, you two!" It was our upstairs neighbor. When she found out we were in the midst of a proposal, she was very embarrassed.

We went right back into the pawn shop and bought the diamond ring. For my birthday the next month, he also gave me the ring with the tourmaline! I always tease him that he could have had me for the $129 tourmaline ring rather than the much-more-expensive diamond ring!

I was totally flabbergasted. All I could do was grab him for a big kiss.

That was March 1989. We were married that May. We're still inseparable, and I still wear both the diamond ring and the tourmaline one, along with several others he has given me over the years.

The Universe Conspires

- Patty Mooney
New & Unique Videos
www.newuniquevideos.com

My story is quite unusual in that my husband Mark proposed what was essentially a honeymoon before he ever proposed marriage.

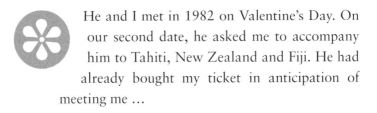

He and I met in 1982 on Valentine's Day. On our second date, he asked me to accompany him to Tahiti, New Zealand and Fiji. He had already bought my ticket in anticipation of meeting me …

You see, nine months prior to Valentine's Day, he had made a wish to the Universe: "To meet my soulmate on or before Valentine's Day." So when he saw me on the balcony of La Paloma Theater in Encinitas, California on Valentine's Day, he knew I was The One.

On St. Patrick's Day, he and I went shopping for backpacks, tents, etc. On April Fool's Day, we stepped aboard a flight for Tahiti.

We spent three months backpacking and hitchhiking around Tahiti, Fiji, and

New Zealand, where I knew that I had fallen in love with Mark. Almost as an afterthought, he and I married on our mountain bikes in Cleveland National Forest in July 1987.

And we have been living happily ever after, since then.

Fasten Your Seatbelts

- Paul Dearing

My sister Sheila was dating her dance instructor Allen. They were headed out of town to dance together in a competition and agreed to meet at the airport. When Sheila arrived at the gate, Allen was waiting for her and they boarded the plane together.

The flight took off, and the moment the seatbelt sign turned off, a man, a stranger, walked up the aisle to my sister and asked, "Is your name Sheila?" When she answered "Yes," the stranger handed her a long-stemmed red rose and returned to his seat without explanation.

This act was repeated eleven more times. Eleven more strangers from various parts of the plane walked up to my sister, handed her a red rose, and returned to their seats. Allen then took the last rose out of its hiding place, handed it to my stunned sister and asked, "Will you marry me?"

Allen had arrived at the gate early with a dozen roses, hoping he could put his plan in place before my sister arrived. His original intent was to have a flight attendant deliver the roses mid-flight. However, the flight attendant refused, citing security regulations.

Fashioning a hasty plan B, Allen enlisted eleven fellow passengers, all total strangers, to help him. He told them all Sheila's seat number and instructed them to take turns in delivering the roses. Allen enlisted his eleventh co-conspirator and concealed the twelfth rose just as Sheila arrived at the gate.

> A stranger walked up the aisle and asked, "Is your name Sheila?"

Even though she had declined to participate, the flight attendant shared with the pilots that there was to be a proposal onboard. Shortly after the last rose was delivered and Allen had asked Sheila to marry him, the captain asked loudly over the PA, "Well, what did she say?"

Sheila's enthusiastic "Yes!" resulted in a round of applause from the entire plane. The captain added his congratulations.

When Sheila and Allen were married the next summer, they chose July 27, or 7/27, as their wedding day to allow them to continue the airline theme, after becoming engaged on a 727.

Wedding Planning

Gone to the Dogs

- Catherine & Doug Baker

We live in Arizona but planned a destination wedding on a beautiful beach in La Jolla, California. Luckily, my Maid of Honor lived nearby in San Diego so I was able to have a lot of things for the wedding shipped to her house to avoid having to drive out with a carload of favors and accessories.

One of the items I had sent to her were our chocolate seashell favors. The company's website had very lengthy and specific instructions about how to ship and store and handle the seashells. For instance, they couldn't be refrigerated or handled without gloves and needed to be kept in plastic baggies at a constant 75 degrees. Very high-maintenance!

With shipping and the cooler pack they came in, these simple favors ending up being quite expensive, so I sent our Maid of Honor an email detailing the instructions for caring for the chocolates. The trouble started when the chocolates shipped on a Friday instead of the Monday before the wedding. The Maid of Honor called at 4:30 p.m. on Friday to say that they still hadn't arrived at her office and she was due to leave in less than an hour. If she didn't get them in the next 45 minutes, they would be stuck in a hot UPS storage facility for who knows how long over the weekend.

We spent the next 45 minutes tracking down the truck the favors were on and the Maid of Honor had to chase the driver through the streets of San Diego to get the package in time. Thankfully the chocolates were intact and not melted. She rushed them home to a cool area of her house and babied them for a week until our wedding day.

> I knew something was wrong the second we walked into the hotel room ...

The day before the wedding, the Maid of Honor brought her things over to the hotel where we were getting married so we could spend the day together. She brought everything I'd had shipped to her throughout the planning process, such as my shoes, hairpiece, and the seashell-shaped chocolates. She also brought her dog, a Pomeranian.

We spent a lovely day having brunch by the beach, drinking mimosas, and getting manicures and pedicures. We were laughing and really enjoying ourselves when we got back to the hotel that evening.

I knew something was wrong the second we walked into the hotel room. There were little bits of Styrofoam everywhere. That's when my Maid of Honor said, "Oh my god, I think my dog ate the chocolates."

Sure enough, the dog had torn open the Styrofoam cooler and gone to town on my chocolate seashells. I didn't have much chance to grieve over the fact that my pretty (and expensive) wedding favors were ruined, however, because the dog started vomiting all over the hotel room floor and wouldn't stop. Although I was upset, I sucked it up and said, "I think we should take the dog to the vet." Good thing we did, too, because apparently, chocolate is poisonous to dogs!

The good news is, the dog lived and my Maid of Honor showed up just in time for the rehearsal dinner speeches. When I toasted her, I made sure to thank her for taking such good care of my chocolates — better watch than she had kept over her dog!

Easier to Elope

- Courtney and Darrin Hunter

I joke with people that you *can* plan a wedding in two weeks, including finding the dress! And that they should elope. Ha!

Our story goes that we planned our wedding a year in advance but had to basically re-plan it in two weeks. I hate change and try to avoid it, but then there's Murphy's Law. If it's going to happen, it will happen to me! Because of this I have learned that things are out of my control and I have to let life take its course.

The trouble started when an ex-boyfriend (we hadn't dated in years but were really good friends and hung out in the same crowd) proceeded to tell me that he was in love with me. He showed up at my house later that evening to continue to profess his undying love and tell me that I was marrying the wrong person and he was the one for me. Yikes! That sure sends you into a tailspin.

I hadn't really heard from the gal at the catering company all summer and finally got in touch with her about three weeks prior to the wedding requesting a final menu and reception layout. I'd told her to have creative freedom with the menu since neither of us are picky eaters. At our original meeting we'd asked her if a budget of $10,000 for food would be sufficient. She assured us yes, but two weeks prior to the wedding, she sent me a menu that looked fantastic but the price was $27,000! Ack! The phone calls began, to her, her boss, her boss's boss, etc. We ended up with fantastic food, but what an ordeal.

> I tell brides not to worry about the little things; no one will remember your pink shoes or what types of cheese you served.

Then, one and a half weeks prior to the wedding, my wedding dress was stolen out of my car in a matter of 15 minutes! I was on my way to a fitting and stopped to run a quick errand. They also took my perfect pink shoes! The place I'd bought my dress from sold me the sample gown, but for the exact same price that I'd bought the original one for — no discount for a dirty dress. They didn't clean it and didn't really seem to care. They actually told me I was lucky they'd sell it to me.

That same week, I received a call from my linen company saying that the linens we'd picked out and ordered months prior were not going to get in until 3 days *after* my wedding. Back I went to pick out new linens.

Then, the week of my wedding, my florist called to tell me that my flowers arrived but they had yellow centers instead of black.

The final disaster was when my guestbook, which I'd made, didn't get put out at my reception. I had spent a lot of time and money creating it, and after the wedding I had an empty book.

Despite the obstacles, the day of our wedding was great and I enjoyed every minute of it! The food was fantastic, my dress looked great, flowers were awesome, groom was handsome, and everyone had fun.

I tell future brides not to worry about the little things; no one will remember your flowers, your pink shoes, your linens, what types of cheese you served. They will remember the laughs, the fun, and the love that was shared that day.

Had I made a huge deal about any of the above, I doubt our day would have been as nice, relaxing, and enjoyable as it was. If someone had not heard the stories of what happened the two weeks leading up to the wedding, they would not have been able to tell.

Love, Error & Eros

- Felicia Morgenstern

I'm an author, artist and adventuress. Apparently, I am also a bit thick-headed when the Universe sends me neon signs in an attempt to intervene on my behalf. When I was engaged to be married to the man I thought was my soulmate, I knew exactly where I wanted to tie the knot: AVAM, The American Visionary Arts Museum in Baltimore. I'm a quirky, self-taught artist and AVAM celebrates just that.

I was an anti-bride incarnate. I didn't care about a wedding dress — I ditched wedding white in favor of a raspberry-sorbet number from Bloomingdale's — and left hors d'oeuvres decisions, wedding-cake-picking, and music selection up to others. But I wanted AVAM as my wedding venue, and that was the one area where I refused to budge.

When I took my then-fiancé, now ex-husband, to AVAM to plan our wedding, the exhibition was, shall we say, an interesting one: "Love, Error & Eros," which displayed art with themes like "love scorned" and "love lost." It was as if the fates, the stars, the universe itself aligned to deliver an unsubtle message this would be the unholiest of unions. Unfortunately, I found the love-crossed museum exhibition as a backdrop for my nuptials sublimely hilarious, and we went forward with our museum wedding.

Little did I know our union would indeed quickly proceed from "Love" directly to "Error" while entirely skipping the fun of "Eros." Currently, I am in the final stages of planning my "Unbridaled Shower" to celebrate my divorce! Gal pal guests are wearing their wedding dresses (if they've had the fortune or misfortune) or their most hideous shimmery-mermaid bridesmaids' dresses.

> It was as if the fates, the stars, the universe itself aligned to deliver an unsubtle message.

Moral of the story: When the universe delivers a blunt, neon-marquis sign of a cosmic message pointing to the escape exit, grab a pair of Nikes and run!

Bride in the Weeds

- Susan Songy
  Scentsational Events
  http://scentsationalevents.com

Years ago, I was planning my own wedding on a shoestring budget of $500. Yes, $500! I bought some silk flowers at the dollar store and awkwardly made my bouquet and my bridesmaids' bouquets. I bought my gown at a $99 sale. I planned my reception in the free party room of my girlfriend's apartment building and cooked all the food myself.

The ceremony was to be held in a quaint stone chapel, and the only thing missing were flowers for the ceremony site. My fiancé's best friend John was a naturalist for The Smithsonian, so I had the idea that he could collect some wildflowers for me and place them on either side of the rustic altar, instead of buying us a gift. I pictured charming little daisies, buttercups, maybe a few bluebells ... perfect for the stone chapel. John readily agreed, and everything was set.

The morning of the wedding, my attendants and I were at the chapel, anxiously awaiting the arrival of the altar flowers as the final touch before the ceremony began. My fiancé and his groomsmen were cutting it close and many of the guests were already milling around outside the chapel, waiting to be let in. I went out to greet some of my family members who had driven a considerable distance to attend. As we chatted on the sidewalk, John drove up and unloaded two large arrangements of ... weeds!

> I'm sure my face was every shade of red ...

I stared in disbelief at two plastic containers filled with Goldenrod and Queen Anne's Lace. John explained that these were the only kinds of wildflowers that grew locally in Maryland in August. As he walked up and placed them on the altar, I heard one of my aunts whisper loudly, "Is that GOLDENROD?!"

I was so ashamed; I'm sure my face was every shade of red. Until that moment, I was certain there was no evidence of my limited budget, but the weed-filled buckets were a dead give-away. That episode is probably why I later took floral design classes and became an events florist! I must have been trying to spare other brides the humiliation of a weed-filled event!

Photog Gone Rogue

- Meghann Scherrer

Exactly three months before my June 2009 wedding I learned that my photographer had gone completely rogue. A coworker had asked me about my photographer and wanted to see who I was using. Forgetting his website, I Googled him. What came up was not his website but rather a forum with at least 30 people claiming that this guy had completely swindled them and owed them proofs, service and money!

I pored over my emails and paperwork, only to realize that the last correspondence I had from him was months prior when I had hounded him for weeks to get just two pictures from our engagement session. Periodically, I had sent him emails over the holidays to check in, but never heard back. I didn't think anything of it until I found that forum thread. I realized then that I didn't have my engagement pictures, the disc he promised us or the prints he promised us. To add insult to injury, we had not only paid him a down payment but also a first installment of several thousand dollars. That very day, I started combing the Internet trying to find photographers in my area who would happen to be free on a Saturday evening in the busiest wedding month of the year.

My mother and I continued to contact him via email and phone. Still no luck. We sent him a registered letter to his last known address as well as the address listed online. The first one came back within 10 days saying that no one was there (the house was under Sheriff Sale). The second letter, to his mother's house where he was reportedly hiding, was returned to us 20 days later as "refused."

Meanwhile, I spent my weekends trying to complete the regular activities I had planned (I was planning my wedding in Philadelphia on weekends while living in D.C.). I was scurrying between scheduled appointments while on the phone talking with booked photographer after photographer. Finally, I was able to talk to a photographer who not only happened to be free my day, but I would be the last wedding she'd book for the entire year. She sounded fabulous and fit within our already seriously dented photography budget.

It was fate. Isabel March came to our rescue, and our wedding photography fiasco turned into a perfect fairytale. Isabel did a phenomenal job, as you can see on her blog, isabelmarchphotography.com/blog.

Honestly, I can't stop staring at my wedding photos, even three-plus-months post-W day! It really goes to show that sometimes the worst disasters are blessings in disguise!

Caterer Calamity

- Chrissy Slater

My husband and I got married in October 2009 and thankfully everything turned out beautifully. It had its small glitches, but no one would ever have known. The one major problem we had was having to change the caterer two weeks before the wedding! When you are expecting 165 guests, it's no small feat to find someone to feed them on short notice.

With 200 invited guests, we started planning our wedding a year and a half before, and we were ahead of schedule throughout the planning process. We had found a caterer with delicious food who had been in the business for over 20 years. Sounds like someone you can trust right?

When we decided to choose him as our caterer, we asked to see the contract. His reply: "I don't worry with contracts. My word is my bond and it is as good as gold." My fiancé, being very business smart, insisted on one in order to protect us and the caterer. We had to type it up ourselves but felt that everything would be perfect. We put in the contract that any changes could be made up to two weeks out and that the final headcount was due two weeks before the wedding, which is more than fair.

Two months before the wedding, I attempted to take just one of the hors d'oeuvres off the menu. My grandfather, a dairy farmer, wanted to provide the cheese himself. It shouldn't have been an issue since I still had over a month and a half to make any changes with the caterer. He caused such a stink about it though, I just had him change it to something else rather than remove it from the cost.

Then, two weeks before the wedding, I called to give him the final headcount of 165 and he flipped out on me! He said I was trying to nickel and dime him and that our guest list was supposed to be 200. Most vendors know that all of your invited guests will not come to the wedding. You are lucky if you have 65 percent of the invited guest list; we had 80 percent. This is the reason for a final headcount!

> We had to type up the contract ourselves but felt that everything would be perfect ...

I got upset with the caterer for trying to break the contract and the way he was talking with me. As I was crying on the phone he said it would probably be best if we found a different caterer because he didn't think he could make me happy. When he said that I knew I couldn't count on him to do what he had promised; he was irrational.

So that very same day I worked hard to find a dependable

caterer. And I did! He not only worked with us to create the same menu, but he saved us money and had his own contract. The funny thing was the old caterer called back the next day and tried to change his mind again and force us to use him. He realized that while he had been worried about losing the money for 35 guests, he was now going to get nothing. His loss; he never should have counted his chickens before they hatched. Guest lists always fluctuate and usually decrease. Lesson learned for him!

Since we were past the two-week deadline in the contract, it was too late to try and force us to use him. And it was fortunate for us! The new caterer was trustworthy and did a wonderful job. The lesson? Always require wedding vendors to have a contract!

Destination Wedding Disaster

- Shaina Rance

When my fiancé asked me to marry him, I was ecstatic. He is everything I could have dreamed of in a man, and I am still wondering how I got so lucky. What I didn't anticipate was one year of the most bizarre circumstances possible leading up to our wedding. While we are slightly superstitious, if we actively believed in bad omens we would have been convinced that all the forces of man and nature were against us! Dramatic, maybe, but see if you don't agree.

First, when and where to get married? We decided on one of our favorite places, Puerto Vallarta, Mexico in May of 2009. We found a travel agent who booked us and 32 guests on Conquest Vacations.

Then, like a dream come true, I found a local wedding store in our small town that carried the wedding gown designer I favored, and I ordered the dress. The whole process took about ten minutes.

After feeling good about our plans, it was February when things began to fall apart.

We received a panicked phone call from our travel agent. "Shaina, are you sitting down?" she asked. "I am sorry to inform you that your tour operator has gone into receivership. Oh, and good luck getting your money back. There is nothing I can do."

When my fiancé's brother-in-law got wind of this, he was like a bulldog! He got the money back for all 32 of our guests. So, crisis averted! We called the travel agent and booked with another tour operator — and they were even a little cheaper than the original.

> We received a panicked phone call from our travel agent. "Are you sitting down?" she asked.

We were getting set to leave April 30, when another call came in from our poor travel agent. "Shaina," she said, again, "Are you sitting down? Better yet, are you sitting down with a glass of wine?"

Swine flu had hit Mexico.

She told us all flights had been cancelled into Mexico. She said, "I can book you elsewhere, but all of your guests already in Mexico will have to stay there. No one will risk taking them due to swine flu."

My family was already in Mexico. No airline would take them anywhere. There went my dream wedding.

So, instead of Mexico, we ended up in Hawaii. Myself, my Maid of Honor and 19 of my fiancé's relatives. Not a relaxing trip, but it was OK. Not my dream wedding, but we made the best of it. Time to regroup and plan a local wedding for when we got back.

We set the date for August 15, 2009 — a local affair so all our friends and family could celebrate together. What could go wrong?

A couple of weeks after this plan was in place, my fiancé and I were in the bank putting each others' names on our accounts. As we were waiting for our account manager I happened to glance down at the newspaper on the table. I began to laugh hysterically and my poor fiancé was at a loss. He was probably thinking I had finally cracked and lost my marbles. He looked at the paper and saw the headline: "Wedding store fire! All is lost in local store!" Want to guess where my wedding dress was?

We snuck off to Las Vegas shortly after and thankfully seem to have used up our bad luck on the wedding, as our marriage has been wonderful!

Wedneck
Wedding Contest

- Paris Raedine Starr Byrum
  & Jonathan James Byrum

When my husband and I first moved up to Idaho, we were only two months engaged and were planning on having a home wedding in California. But we decided to enter a contest at the Idaho Summer Festival, just for fun and to meet people. The contest was called the Wedneck Wedding Contest. We thought it would be fun to laugh and work together in this crazy contest.

The event we were competing in was to have Idaho's largest wedding. Couples would compete against one another for prizes during the events leading up to the wedding. The winning couple had to be married at Sandy Downs the day after the contest. This very unique wedding entailed being married in front of the festival crowd, with an Elvis impersonator as the officiant and a performance after the wedding. The couple would begin their reception by receiving a Dodge Durango from *Idaho Wedding Guide*, plus 30 tickets to the upcoming Rock the Falls concert.

We drove 9 hours to get to Sandy Downs, where the contest was taking place, and signed in. There were supposedly 20 couples signing up, but when we got there, we only were competing against 6! So our game faces were on. At first we were thinking, *We never win anything*, but with that few couples everyone could win a good prize, just for participating.

We participated in 10 elimination events that included a Garter Removal Contest; Wedding Music Contest, where couples work together to name songs; the Bridal Bouquet Contest, where the groom gets points for throwing his bridal bouquet closest to a bullseye; an Obstacle Course; a Wedding Cake Eating Contest; Wedding Rings in a Hay Stack Contest; Trash the Tux and Wedding Dress Contest, where each couple has ten shots each with a paintball gun to hit a target; Kiss the Pig Contest; a Wedding Planning game, where the couple has to work together to complete a series of typical planning tasks while one person is blindfolded; and a Chocolate Covered Hot Dog and Dill Pickle Eating Contest.

> This very unique wedding entailed being married in front of the festival crowd, with an Elvis impersonator as the officiant.

While competing, we quickly realized we were one of the top three couples. We were super excited! We really wanted to win first place in every competition so we could get married and win that car!

By the next day, we were exhausted because of all 10

events and because we were camping out. They called all the couples to the stage to make the announcement about which couple would be getting married the very next day. We were in the top two, and as they announced second place, we just knew we were the winners!

The next day we got married by Elvis and took home our new Dodge Durango. The odd thing was, while we did get the car, we didn't end up getting the 30 concert tickets. I guess the event planners didn't really have their act together. But we had tons of fun participating in the games and, of course, winning. And we'll be having a traditional wedding for our friends and family in a few months!

Everything That Can Go Wrong, Will

- Scott and Christie Sommers

We had heard that all wedding planning is stressful, but sometimes it can be downright disastrous. First, we went through four ministers due to retirements at the church. Next, our invitations were wrong eight different times, which made it so they were late being sent out.

Then, the bridesmaids' dresses were discontinued, which would not have been a big deal except Christie's best friend of 10 years emailed her a few weeks before the wedding and said she was not coming, and did not even give a reason. The store also ordered wraps for the dresses instead of the sashes we paid for. Christie's dress was altered too small, as well!

Right before we were supposed to meet with the organist to choose our music, our dog attacked Christie and she ended up in the ER and had to get stitches in her arm!

Next, the beautiful golf course where we booked our rehearsal dinner temporarily closed due to a neural virus, and we had to move the location of the dinner at the last minute.

With all these setbacks, we had fallen a bit behind in planning, so our wedding bands were not even finished being made in time for the wedding.

The actual day went even worse! The flowers came and Christie's bouquet was pink instead of white. The bridesmaids' flowers were wrapped in purple instead of white and had four roses instead of nine. The church arrangements came, and they looked like they belonged at a funeral. Even though the florist eventually fixed Christie's bouquet, she cried, ruined her makeup, and therefore did not get any photos with her bridesmaids because there was no time. Luckily, Christie's parents were able to get some money back from the florist because we had taken pictures of the flowers when he did the sample bouquets.

> The church arrangements came, and they looked like they belonged at a funeral.

Christie also forgot to break in her wedding shoes before the big day, and they were so awful she ended up changing them halfway down the stairs on her way to the aisle.

The photographer proved to be a disaster, too. She messed up countless times during the wedding, including trying to send the second photographer home after three hours. We paid big money to have two, so I had to fight with her to get the assistant to stay. After the wedding, the photographer claimed to never have taken certain pictures that we had specifically requested, such as a photo of Christie and her mom. We were just devastated, but suddenly, six months later she magically "found" the pictures she told us she never took! Really, she Photoshopped pictures together to make it look like she took them! We tried to get some money back from her, but unfortunately, without a written shot list, she refused to take responsibility for the missing shots. There's a good lesson: Always write out a shot list for your photographer, and be sure to pay the extra money for a real professional.

And the lesson that is most important: Love your husband or wife. Know he or she loves you. Know you can get through anything together, even if it is the big craziness surrounding the wedding day!

Frozen Solid

- Penny Tubbs

I had a wonderful wedding planned for 300 people over Thanksgiving weekend, but the morning of the wedding a freak freezing rain hit the area. It came down as rain and froze upon contact. My car's defroster was not working, and I had trouble seeing through the icy windshield.

That's when I found out the minister and most of the wedding party could not get to the wedding. In the end, our wedding for 300 ended up being less than 50. Not only did we have lots of cake and food leftover, but we weren't able to travel to our honeymoon.

We ended up staying in a room at the hotel where we had the reception. We had given all our guests the location of the room so it could be used for coats and handbags during the reception, not knowing we would be spending the night in it. So the room was not quite a romantic suite for the newlyweds. Oh, and our friends thought it was funny to come by and knock on our door all night long, because they too were not able to travel home. Not exactly the wedding and honeymoon we had planned for.

Needless to say, a page from the local paper with the headline about the freak weather is what we put in the front of our wedding book.

Nightmare New Orleans Nuptials

- Melanie Young

What Mother of the Bride did not impact, Mother Nature did for my New Orleans destination wedding in March 2007.

First, a freak Nor'easter blew into New York early on the Friday morning before the wedding. Thirty of my wedding guests, including four from Europe, were left stranded in New York since the three major airports cancelled all flights and would not re-book for the next day. So, I lost 1/3 of my wedding party. That same day I wisely hired a videographer to tape the wedding to share it with everyone who missed it.

Then, three hours before the wedding, my mother tripped and fell while watching the Saint Patrick's Day Parade, hurt her leg and had to be sedated. She went through the entire wedding drugged, and my father was hysterical. I am an only child and my mother has spent the last 15 years trying to find me a husband and dreaming of "starring" in my wedding as Mother of the Bride.

As if it couldn't get worse, the photographer lost the memory card with all of the wedding portrait and family photos. We have no wedding portraits, just crazy, inebriated "party shots."

I did manage, the day after my wedding to pull together a "re-enactment" dinner party in New York for the friends and family who did not make the wedding. My new husband, David, and I wore our wedding clothes again, shipped all the wedding favors back to New York and showed the wedding on a large screen. It wasn't the same as being in New Orleans but it shared the spirit and made everyone feel they were there in some way.

> She went through the entire wedding drugged, and my father was hysterical.

Putting Out Fires

- Jolie and Nate Downs

I had many mishaps with my wedding. They started with the dress. The woman who ordered my dress was much older, most likely the mother or grandmother of the shop owner, and she ordered my dress about four sizes too large. They altered the dress but when I tried it on the day before the wedding it was still too big. They told me to use tape. Not what you want to deal with the day before your wedding during the hot season.

Then, the bridesmaids got their hair done and they all hated it. Six women complaining and groaning to a bride who has to wear the too-big dress. Ugh.

The day of the wedding was hot, hot, hot. The church was sweltering as the air conditioning had broken. I had to wipe the sweat pouring down my husband's face during the ceremony!

After the ceremony, we walked out of the church and the wedding party had butterflies to let off but many of them had died in the heat. Nate and

I let off a pair of doves, one of which promptly pooped directly on my ring finger, below my wedding ring.

When we got to the ceremony, more people showed up than we had seats for, there weren't enough beef entrees for the number of people who claimed to have ordered it, and many other friends who didn't have an invite decided to crash the wedding. Oh, and then one of the centerpieces on the table caught on fire. That was exciting!

> We let off a pair of doves, one of which promptly pooped directly on my ring finger.

But in the end, I married the man I love with all of my family and friends (plus a few extra friends) present, and that is what really mattered. I told myself I wouldn't allow anything to bother me, I was going to enjoy my day, and I had so much fun!

Your wedding is one day. You put so much time and preparation into it, and it would be an absolute waste if you worry about all the little details that just don't matter. Your wedding day is over in the blink of an eye, so slap a smile on your face, laugh at the mishaps and enjoy the day!

Wedding Planner to the Rescue

- Catharine Han
  Your Dream Wedding & Events
  www.dreamweddingwisconsin.com

In 2006, I worked with a very cute couple who knew each other since high school. They had never really thought about getting married because to them, they already were. However, the bride's grandmother was very sick and her wish was to see her granddaughter get married. So they hired me to plan a wedding in 6 months.

The time came for the wedding. I was setting up the ceremony when several things started to go wrong. First, one of the mothers came to me saying a couple of the boutonnieres were missing. I took a rose and greenery from two bridesmaids' bouquets, went into my emergency bag for floral tape, and created the boutonnieres.

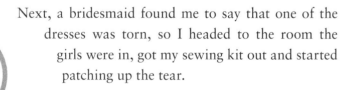

Next, a bridesmaid found me to say that one of the dresses was torn, so I headed to the room the girls were in, got my sewing kit out and started patching up the tear.

Once the ceremony started I headed over to the reception to meet with the vendors. They all arrived on time; however — and I never thought

I would see this — when the baker came, he started to put together the cake. He set down the first tier, no problem ... then, as he was about to put on the second tier, it slipped out of his hands and landed on the floor. He looked at me and said he was sorry. When he called the bakery to get another tier, the person on the phone told him that they did not have any cakes available. So, as fast as possible, I headed over to the nearest grocery store, hoping they would have cakes. I bought a few cakes with floral designs. When I got back to the reception site, the baker had left. He told one of the waitresses that he could not stay because he had to deliver two other cakes and that he was sorry. So I was stuck putting together this cake.

> I was just praying that this incident would not ruin the couple's night.

Carefully, I stacked the cakes I had bought on top of the first tier that was already there and then set the top tier that was left from the baker on top of all that. Somehow, the cake looked great! It did not look like the cake the couple had ordered but now it was taller and had square and round tiers. I also called the bakery to let them know that the baker had just left and that they would be seeing me during the week about this.

When it came time for the bride and groom to enter the reception hall, I was just praying that this cake incident would not ruin the couple's night. I looked for their reactions — they looked surprised but I couldn't tell how they were really feeling. The bride finally came over and whispered, "This is not the cake we ordered ... it looks bigger and better and I love it!" So, I decided not to tell her what had happened. The couple went on with the rest of the day, relaxed and enjoyed themselves; however, there was one other thing in store for me.

During dinner, the bridal party had gotten drunk, and before the dancing started, a fight broke out between the bridal party and a couple of the guests! When I heard of this from the Maid of Honor, who was not drunk, I had to go over and break up the fight. I reminded them that this was their friend's special day, and they were ruining it. I told them to fix themselves up before going back into the wedding.

To this day, I am pretty sure the couple has no idea these things had happened at their wedding, which I am thankful for. The funniest part is, I have gotten several referrals out of that wedding, including the bridal party — I have planned all eight of the bridal party members' weddings! I have also planned many of their guests' weddings.

This wedding was one I will never forget. Since then, I have fixed a lot more dresses, made a lot more boutonnieres and bouquets, and much more. This wedding taught about more than just being a wedding planner — it taught me about being ready for anything to happen!

Gown

Wedding Gown Countdown

- Sarah Jang

I fell in love with a designer gown but was not convinced that I needed to pay a designer price for what was a very, very simple dress. I felt I could find a similar dress that was more affordable. After several months of looking, I found one the perfect one, but I was ordering a wedding dress in July for a November wedding, thus the store informed me that it was past their 6-month mark for ordering a gown.

Next, I tried to order the gown online. The website would not let the order go through, because, again, I was not ordering 6 months in advance. I called to order, and they still maintained that they could not get the dress in time for my ceremony. I asked to speak to management. I could not convince anyone that it could not possibly take 6 months for a dress that was so simple in design. I asked them to call around and see if there was a floor model of the gown anywhere around the country — even a different size that I could have altered. There wasn't one.

Frustrated, I demanded to know what about making this dress would take so long. I could not get an answer from anyone — the just kept telling me that they needed 6 months. When wedding planning books tell you to order your dress more than 6 months in advance, believe it! I was in a bind.

I finally accepted that there was no way I could convince the company to order the dress in time for the wedding. I also realized that it was too late for *any* of the other dresses I was considering. Ordering a wedding gown was not an option.

I decided to look for a dress off the rack and spent the next two months doing that. Still no luck.

I was really racing against the clock now, so I started thinking about making the dress myself. My fiancé said he would not marry me if he had to live with me while I was trying to make my own wedding dress.

So I decided to get the dress made. It was a very simple, basic sheath design, so I thought it would be easy. I found a dressmaker who said she could do it in time for the wedding. I met with the designer, showed her a picture of the dress, and she said it was no problem. She said that she did not need a pattern, that she would just drape it, and that the design was simple enough where it would be easy to sew. She said all I needed to do was to buy the fabric.

For my next adventure, I went shopping at the fabric store. No store had the fabric I was looking for in the color I wanted. Everything felt cheap and flimsy or was exorbitantly expensive. I went online to order fabric. At this point, I did not have time to get a swatch, and I ended up rush-ordering 5 yards of the wrong fabric. Which was non-returnable ... I then rush-ordered the correct fabric. Great! I gave both sets of fabric to the dressmaker who said she would hold onto the wrong fabric and see if there was another client who would want to buy the material from me. (I never did get it back.)

Over the next weeks, I went in for several fitting. During the fittings I noted that things were off about the dress — seams were not clean and even, the dress did not drape properly, and other little details were off. For a simple dress that is all out clean lines, cut and drape, these issues made a big difference. When I mentioned this, the designer said that all the details would be cleaned up for the final fitting and pick-up.

I had my final fitting two weeks before the wedding, and the dress was not in good shape. I honestly could have made that dress in a week and done a better job. I considered doing just that. I also thought about not accepting the dress, but I had already spent so much money on the material. After all, the dress was already done, and I had no back up.

I spent the next week fretting over the dress. Finally, I couldn't stand it — even though he was not supposed to see my gown before the wedding, I asked my fiancé to tell me, honestly, what he thought of the dress. I tried it on for him, and he said that it was a nice design but poorly made.

He actually wanted to call and yell at the dressmaker (who soon after went out of business), but I assured him that it wouldn't do any good at that point.

I had one week to get a wedding dress.

I had just heard about J.Crew's newly launched bridal collection, so I went on their website. At that time, they had just a few classic, inexpensive gowns. I ordered two dresses and had them FedExed. One design was almost exactly like the initial dress that I wanted, but I had ordered the wrong size. I didn't have time to exchange it, so I ordered a third dress in the correct size and style two days before I was supposed to leave for my out-of-town wedding.

I had J.Crew overnight the gown to arrive on the day before I was supposed to fly out for the wedding. I stayed home from work all day waiting for the FedEx truck. I started to get nervous that I would be in the bathroom for 2 minutes, not hear the door and miss my package. I went outside and posted signs on every door for the delivery man saying, "I HAVE TO HAVE THAT PACKAGE. IT HAS MY WEDDING DRESS AND I AM FLYING OUT TOMORROW! I AM HOME! IF FOR SOME REASON I DO NOT ANSWER THE DOOR, IT'S BECAUSE I AM IN THE BATHROOM. PLEASE LEAVE IT AT THE DOOR!" The FedEx guy must have thought I was crazy.

But in the end, I got the dress, it fit perfectly, and we left for our wedding the next day. *Thank god* for J.Crew bridal.

Dry Clean Only

- Kathy Byrum
Dream Wedding and Event Planners
www.dreamweddingplanners.com

I planned and coordinated an exquisite tented wedding reception at a private home in South Rockwood, Michigan. The bride and groom had been married in New York earlier, and the bride's sister threw them this reception for their Michigan family and friends.

When the bride arrived in Michigan, she took her dress to a dry cleaner that advertised gown cleaning and preservation. When she picked it up the day before the event, it looked like they had thrown her couture wedding gown into a washing machine and scorched it with a hand iron!

The bride and her sister called me in tears at 4:30 p.m. on Friday, and the reception was due to begin at 5 p.m. the next day. I sent them to a local couture gown designer, Katerina Bocci. I thought, *If anyone can make a brand-new gown in less than one day, Katerina can. This is our only shot.*

Katerina cancelled her meetings and called in her designers and, sure enough, they made the bride a new dress exactly like the ruined gown, finishing at 2 a.m. on Saturday morning!

When the bride arrived to pick up her new dress, Katerina had a glass of wine, soft music, and a masseuse there to relax her before her Big Day. You wouldn't have thought it was possible, but the wedding was saved.

No Horsing Around

- Darius Kaufmann
  Bagpipes for All Occasions
  www.gigmasters.com/folk/BagpipesForAllOccasions

I have been a professional bagpiper in the tri-state area for 15 years, playing for weddings, parties, and more. Once, I was playing bagpipes for a wedding at the Ladies Pavilion in Central Park, NY. The couple had both flown in all the way from Scotland, and the photographer and I were waiting at the curb as the bride and her father pulled up in a horse-drawn carriage. The bride arrived wearing a beautiful creamy-satin dress, which went stunningly with her flawless figure.

As they stepped to the curb, the photographer positioned himself to start taking pictures. Suddenly, we heard a very loud sound like rushing water. We all stopped for a second, perplexed .... Then the bride's mouth opened and her face froze in an expression of utter horror. I followed her gaze and saw that the horse was peeing, no gushing, all over the back of the bride's dress! I had never seen a horse pee like that. It was like a waterfall, and not just for a second — this was about a 20-second gush. We were all frozen for a half-minute or so, then realized what had happened as the bride was shrieking. Then, thankfully, everyone started laughing.

Now, the photographer had a gimmick of capturing a "New York moment" with all his wedding clients, such as photographing them eating a hotdog from a street vendor. Immediately I said to him: "Quick, get a shot! That's a real New York moment!"

The ceremony was happening immediately, and they were already a little late, so there was no time to even try to blot the dress. Thank goodness the short ceremony was in an outside gazebo, so no one sat down and the couple faced outward toward the guests. The wet backside of her gown wasn't visible to anyone. Good thing the horse was behind her and not in front!

> We were all frozen for a half-minute or so, then realized what had happened as the bride was shrieking.

Despite the initial horror, the bride went right ahead with the whole wedding, sopping dress and all. And, it was a beautiful wedding.

Not Just a Sprinkle

- Debbie Flores

Planning a wedding is an intricate and stressful process, but most brides will agree that once they have their dress, everything else is smooth sailing. They can't explain the feeling except to say that they just know when they've found the perfect dress. Many times it brings them to tears, or their friend, sister, or mother who has agreed to come along.

On the Big Day, you can expect that something will inevitably go awry, or at the very least, different from the way you had envisioned it. But what happens when the one thing that you counted on being perfect is the thing that goes horribly wrong?

I am in charge of group room sales at a major hotel. I assist the brides from the beginning stages of the room block process until checkout. This bride, "Sandy," requested 10 rooms for her out-of-town guests, and two suites. The wedding was on a Saturday and the bride was to spend Friday night in the room so that she could start getting ready bright and early. She and the groom would also be spending the wedding night in said suite. The groom had an additional suite for Friday night, which he would use to get ready the morning of the wedding.

Everything was going according to plan. The contract for the room block was signed, reservations were made and, before we knew it, the guests were checking in. The bride arrived at the hotel that evening and had sweet dreams in her soft hotel bed.

She awoke the next morning anxious and a little nervous, but with high hopes for the most important day of her life. The makeup artist and hairdresser arrived at 8 a.m., right on time. The wedding was not until 2, but she wanted to be ready with enough time to avoid rushing. By 10 a.m., with hair and makeup in place, Sandy was ready to try on the dress. The strapless dress was white, crisp, and had a train that was quite long. It did not fit in the closet, so Sandy found a place to hang it — the fire sprinkler!

Little did she know that a few wrinkles would be the least of her concerns ...

The nervous bride hung the dress from the fire sprinkler to avoid it getting wrinkled, but little did she know that a few wrinkles would be the least of her concerns. As she tugged on her dress to release it from the hanger, she broke the safety feature on the sprinkler and set off the high-powered water main. The sheer power from the water pressure threw Sandy back into the arms of her sister and Maid of Honor. The putrid water exploded all over the white dress that still hung from the sprinkler system, which now showered the entire room, including the two 46-inch plasma televisions.

Upon yanking on the sprinkler, the fire alarms were automatically triggered. The fire department was on its way and you could hear the sirens in the background. The water leaked down two floors and ruined the suites below.

Sandy was hysterical: crying, soaking wet, hair ruined, and mascara running down her face — more from the water than her tears. Her dress, *the* perfect dress, was ruined. With only four hours before the ceremony time, she turned to the hotel for help.

If there was a Nobel Prize for wedding-dress restoration, he earned it.

The manager on duty ran up to the room to check on the "fire." It was not until then that he realized there were no flames, and he would have to put out a different kind of fire. The concierge called a nearby cleaner in hopes of restoring the dress. Even if they couldn't get it looking brand new, maybe it would be good enough to wear; after all, she didn't have a back-up wedding dress! The entire wedding revolved around this one important detail.

The only available cleaner drove approximately 20 miles to pick up the ailing dress. He drove it back to the shop and worked on it for almost two hours in an attempt to remove all the stains. He did a magnificent job — if there was a Nobel Prize for wedding-dress restoration, he earned it. The dress was 90 percent restored and the few tiny remaining specks were like battle scars left behind from the war between the bride and the fire sprinkler.

The dress was delivered to a sedated Sandy, with only 30 minutes before the ceremony start time. In an unexpected act of kindness, the cleaner refused to charge her for his services. He felt it would be wrong to take advantage of the situation.

The hotel did not share his sentiment. The labor-intensive cleanup of the six rooms ruined by the water, plus the cost of replacing all the damaged furniture, brought the bride and groom's final bill to approximately $8,000. Her fiancé was happy to pay it and grateful that it didn't amount to more than that. By the end of the evening, it was no more than a story to tell with the happy ending every bride hopes for.

To all of the ladies out there reading this, the moral of the story is: Don't hang anything from a water sprinkler, especially not your wedding dress. It will cost you in more ways than one!

Wedding Party

Best Man or Worst Man?

- Bethany Bledsoe

I think it's smart to expect that your wedding will include mishaps, but you anticipate that you'll brush them off. Realistically, they should pale in comparison to the beauty of your wedding day. However, my fiancé's Best Man made one of the biggest slipups I can imagine, and it nearly ruined my reception.

The ceremony really was the single most special moment of my life. Seeing the way my fiancé looked at me when I started to walk down the aisle just reinforced that I was and am the most wonderful person in the world to him. However, the Best Man seemed to forget that! During his toast at the reception, he got a little distracted (maybe a little whiskey was involved, too?) and called me my fiancé's ex-girlfriend's name — twice!! He literally said, "We are all so happy that Eric and _____ ended up together."

The first time, I almost didn't believe I'd heard him right, but an uncomfortable murmur was going around the room. The second time he called me her name, I almost fell out of my chair. The worst part was, I looked over at my new husband and he was just trying to stifle a laugh. I couldn't believe it; I was mortified. No one spoke up for at least a minute of awful silence until finally an elderly friend of my parents shouted out, "Her name is Bethany!" That broke the tension a little and people started to clap and chuckle.

I, however, was beside myself. I downed my champagne and reached for another glass, and I never drink at all. As soon as the toasts were over I excused myself with my Maid of Honor who tried to comfort me and convince me not to bawl and ruin my perfect makeup. She handed me another glass of champagne to relax me, and I eventually headed back out to the head table with a forced smile on my face.

By that time, my husband had realized his mistake and assured me that he would make the Best Man apologize. In reality, I didn't want him near me. I was sure I would burst into tears. My husband just kept saying over and over, "It was an honest mistake. Let's forget it."

> The Best Man made one of the biggest slipups I can imagine, and it nearly ruined my reception.

And forget it I did, with a fourth glass of champagne. Between crying and the alcohol, things were getting fuzzy. I made it a few songs into the dancing before I had to go into the powder room and lie down on the chaise in there. I must have been gone an hour before I felt ready to go back out again.

Basically, I ended up being the disappearing bride for half of my reception because of that speech. The Best Man did send me a beautiful bouquet of flowers a few weeks after the wedding, to apologize. I guess my only regret is that I let myself get so upset when I should have just grinned and beared it. And that I have sleepy "champagne eyes" in all the photos from the reception!

Dog Day Afternoon

- Gabrielle Yetter

I got married three years ago on Thanksgiving Day. My best friend Patrick and my brother Jonathan and I were at home ready to go to Abbot Hall where I was getting married, since everyone else had already left the house.

The time came to leave and Patrick went outside in the pouring rain to get the car. It wouldn't start. Since he is from England, I thought maybe he was doing something wrong, so I headed out with the umbrella, sat behind the wheel in my wedding dress and tried to start it myself. It still didn't start.

Since it was Thanksgiving and I live in a little New England town, there was no way of getting a taxi. I didn't have my cellphone as it had gone to the hotel where we were staying that night, and none of the neighbors were home. Starting to panic a little, I sat in the car, pushed Patrick and Jonathan out and told them to do what they could to find a car! They ran around the neighborhood in their fancy attire, in the rain, knocking on all the neighbors' doors until they saw someone pulling out of her driveway and pretty much accosted her on the road, telling her we needed a ride to my wedding.

Cheryl, my neighbor, was happy to give us a ride, the only trouble was there was a big black dog in the back of the car, which she explained didn't like men! To avoid getting muddy paw prints on my dress, I sat in the front while Patrick and Jonathan sat in the back with the dog, which was jumping up and down, trying to escape while they chanted "I'm not a man! I'm not a man!" At this point we were all in hysterics. Thankfully, we arrived at Abbott Hall not too much later than planned and I walked down the aisle with a ridiculous smile on my face.

You always have to laugh at whatever happens! I have the best memory and story to tell and will always remember my wedding day with tenderness and laughter. Anyone can have a lovely wedding, but not everyone can have a funny tale to laugh about in the years to come.

Foul-Mouthed Fête

- Kristin Howard
Painted Hills Golf Course

I have worked on some pretty wild weddings, but this one takes the cake — no pun intended. We had a wedding this year for a Bridezilla. She texted, emailed, and phoned the sales manager, the general manager, and food and beverage manager every day for four months prior to her wedding day. She wanted this and that changed one day and the next day she wanted it changed back. Every day she called telling us about some other place that did something different for their brides, and how come we didn't do it that way?! She ordered five kegs of beer to be tapped and poured during the reception. She also demanded coolers of beer for the groom and his groomsmen to be placed in their dressing room, and she wanted wine coolers for herself and her bridal party.

The day of the wedding, they arrived at 10 a.m. with bottles of champagne and orange juice. By noon they had moved on to the wine coolers, beer and Jagermeister (which they smuggled in), and platters of Subway sandwiches they had ordered and had delivered. When it came time for the ceremony, the entire wedding party was wasted! They finished the ceremony, took pictures on the course and came back to the clubhouse for the reception.

After dinner, they decided it would be a good time to toast everyone, which they proceeded to do, for an hour, using the coarsest language imaginable. When the DJ started playing, the aunt of the groom, who was wearing the tightest, shortest dress with the world's biggest shoulder pads, stood on a chair and began dancing. Our security guards asked her to get down, so she raised her dressed and mooned them! The bride came stomping over and screamed at her to leave, using the F-word liberally. Toward the end of the evening, the bride got on the microphone and demanded that all of her "bitches get their asses on the dance floor right *&^%$ now!"

When it finally came time for everyone to leave and the security guards were walking people to the door, the bride started screaming at the policemen, "Don't you know who I am? I am the *&^%$ bride, and I will #$@!^ leave when I am good and ready to $#%@^ leave! I will have your &^%$# badges! I will be on the phone on Monday with your @#$% superiors and I will have your $%$@ jobs!"

Later, when we tried to collect payment for the coolers full of beer and wine coolers, she refused to pay. She also refused to pay for the extra kegs she ordered, denying she had authorized us to tap them.

My GM recently saw her at a charity event and she ran and hid the rest of the night after she saw him. Her new husband came up and started talking to my GM. He never knew that his lovely bride had stiffed us on the bill! He wanted to make it right, but the GM told him it was a learning curve for us, and we now know how to protect ourselves from letting that happen again. The new groom owns a roofing company and our GM mentioned a leak we were experiencing in our roof. So Mr. Bridezilla said he would send his guys over to take care of it.

Our next wedding could not have been more different. The bride had a Mickey Mouse obsession. The centerpieces were Mickey Mouse, she had Mickey and Minnie Mouse dolls hanging from the arch, and she ordered red, yellow and black tablecloths. As a surprise, the bride's mother ordered an ice sculpture, Mickey Mouse, of course, for the cake table, and miniature Mickey and Minnie Mouse sculptures for the head table.

And she did not have a wedding cake, she had cupcakes with Mickey and Minnie Mouse faces on the frosting. The paper napkins were Mickey Mouse, and she had a huge banner of Mickey Mouse hanging on the wall behind the head table.

Then, as another surprise, the grandmother of the bride ordered a Mickey Mouse impersonator to come in and surprise the bride on the dance floor after she and her new husband cut the wedding cupcake. So her first dance was not with her new husband, but with Mickey Mouse. And, yes, they went to Disneyland for their honeymoon!

Impromptu Pool Party

- Rich Amooi
  Hey Mr. DJ
  www.heymrdj.com

After a beautiful wedding ceremony in Santa Cruz, California, the 6 groomsmen and 6 bridesmaids jumped in the wedding party limo to embark on the 40-minute ride to the reception site in Palo Alto. Upon arrival at the hotel, (and many tequila shots later) the Best Man and his buddies thought it would be fun to jump in the swimming pool since it was so hot outside — in their tuxedos.

So they all jumped in, fully clothed. Then, somehow, they convinced the Groom that it was a great idea and he should do it, too. Before the reception had even begun!

The staff at the hotel would not let the guys back into the hotel because they felt the chlorine dripping from their tuxedos would ruin the carpet. So, all of the guys were banging on the windows of the banquet room as the guests watched from the inside.

The bride began to cry hysterically and ran to the bathroom. All of the bridesmaids followed close behind her and a few of them started to cry as well. It was like a scene out of a movie.

Impromptu Pool Party

The Father of the Bride — who was furious — approached the guys outside and told them, "You have one hour to get back here with new, dry tuxedos or I will kill every one of you." They took off in a state of shock. Fortunately for them, there was a Bloomingdale's nearby.

They were not able to find tuxedos; however, they each did buy a new suit, for about $800 apiece! The guys arrived back to the reception exactly one hour later. By then, the bride had stopped crying, but only because she had been drinking while they were gone and was now drunk.

> At the hotel, (and many tequila shots later) they thought it would be fun to jump in the pool ...

The bride actually passed out from the alcohol, but amazingly was able to pull it together to have her First Dance. I still don't know how she did it.

The funniest party was, at the end of the reception, they asked me to make an announcement letting the guests know that the party was going to continue in their hotel room. Unbelievable!

Missing in Action

- Trina Myers
  Affairs Remembered
  www.AffairsRemembered.com

I had a November wedding that totally demonstrated that "anything that can go wrong will go wrong." The wedding was scheduled to begin at 6:30 in the evening, and due to the temperature and the fact that it gets dark very early during that time of year, the guests all arrived early.

Come to find out, the Best Man's van, which was borrowed from a friend, had died on I-95 — along with his cell phone battery. He had in his possession all of the shirts for the males in the wedding party.

Now, I-95 stretches from north of Maryland through the state of Florida, so we had no idea where to find the Best Man. The groom decided to go and look for his friend, only to get lost himself as well.

Meanwhile, on the home front of the wedding and reception, guests waited and began to grow restless. We could only stall for so long. I decided to go ahead and host the cocktail hour before the ceremony, to keep the guests from falling out due to hunger.

After about 1½ hours after the scheduled ceremony start time, I left my two assistants at the venue for crowd control and decided to put on my highway patrolman hat and search for the Best Man and the groom myself. Forty minutes later, I found the groom — and he was less than a half-mile away from the Best Man.

Come to find out he had driven past the Best Man several times, he just didn't recognize the van because it belonged to a friend and the groom was not familiar with the vehicle.

The Best Man hadn't been able to flag down the groom because he had fallen asleep in the van trying to keep warm. The heater had stopped working when the van broke down!

Needless to say, I no longer allow anyone from the male side of the wedding party to pick up formalwear.

After stopping at the nearest gas station, to get the strongest pills allowed without a prescription for a headache the size of Texas, we arrived back at the venue. Guests were in full party mode, dancing and even performing karaoke. Three hours and two very sleepy flower girls later, the ceremony got underway. The officiant based his "For better or for worse" portion on the day's events; the ceremony was not the tearjerker that everyone expected but it made for great comedic material. Everyone agreed, no couple deserved to be married more than these two.

Needless to say, I no longer allow anyone from the male side of the wedding party to pick up formalwear. Once they attend the final fitting and all systems are go, they must bring the shirts and accessories to me.

Management at the venue was very understanding and did not charge the bride and groom for the additional hours, nor did any of the other vendors. For one, the DJ enjoyed the karaoke reception so much that he now recommends it to all of his wedding clients.

I was on the verge of collapse until I realized that all my hard work had not gone to waste. So we missed a couple of cues, and the first dance wasn't the song I recommended. A union took place that day, the couple was happy, and my staff got some additional training that could only have happened in a disaster situation like this!

Princess & The Pooch

- Keith Jagdhuber
Antrim 1844 Country House Hotel
www.antrim1844.com

Just when I thought I had done it all, I offered to watch over the ring bearer, a small dog, for a beautiful, somewhat of a princess, July bride. The day was perfect. Blue skies and a slight breeze. The wedding went off without a hitch. The ring bearer pooch casually walked down the aisle without error — top hat and all.

As the day went on, I kept the little pooch nice and cool in my air-conditioned office. Soon after dinner, I slipped over to check on the dog and found that all was well. While playing with the pooch, my cell rang and I had to go back to the reception immediately — leaving my office door open as I did.

Once I checked on the wedding and found that all was well, I slipped back to the office and yes, of course, the dog had taken off. Running around a 25-acre estate looking for a dog that weighed, at the most, 15 pounds, was not a mission I could take on alone. Before long, I had the entire crew helping me search. The photographer, videographer, the waiters — you name it — I had them all looking for the lost dog. After

30 minutes or so, fearing the worst, I trekked back to the reception to tell the bride and groom the bad news that I had lost their precious dog!

I will never, ever forget the huge sigh of relief when I walked into the ballroom and there was the little pooch "dancing" with the bride and groom. Needless to say, I will never offer to dog sit again.

Ring Bearer Bribe

- James Branum

When our oldest son was getting married in a neighboring state he asked our twin sons, then 4 years old, to each play a role. One carried the ring and the other toted a Bible. 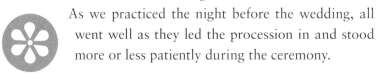 As we practiced the night before the wedding, all went well as they led the procession in and stood more or less patiently during the ceremony.

Then it was time for them to walk in tandem leading the procession down the long carpeted aisle of the church. They took a step or two and looked down the aisle at the open doors. Then they simultaneously ran down the aisle screaming and jumped as far as they could off the front steps. Of course we all laughed. Then we brought them back in and tried to do it again, only the right way this time. As they had been encouraged by our initial laughter, off they were again! We tried a third time ... the same result. My future daughter-in-law looked distraught, our three older sons were appalled, and I was frustrated.

The more we practiced the worse they became. So, we gave up for the evening. The next day I gave it my last, best shot. Lowering my voice as deeply as I could for effect, I looked one and then the other boy in the eye and firmly said, "Boys, if you do it right this time — walk slowly out the aisle and not run and jump off the steps — I'll take you to the zoo." They quickly looked at each other and one of them asked, "What zoo?" I rolled my eyes, not believing I was bargaining with my own boys, and, in desperation said, "Well, I guess the Oklahoma City Zoo." They whispered something to each other and then both gave me their word they'd do it right "just this once." Whew!

> My future daughter-in-law looked distraught, our three older sons were appalled, and I was frustrated.

Well, all went well and they looked so smart in their little tuxedoes proudly marching out in slow, orderly fashion. The whole recessionary line was happy and as I hugged the boys and praised them one asked, "Can we go to the zoo now?" The adults all laughed since the zoo was about 200 miles away. So I replied "Well, not today." My one son blurted out, "We've been had!"

Slip of the Tongue

- Wilson Black
Wilson Black Photography LLC
www.WilsonBlackPhotography.com

I was at the apartment where the bride and her 'maids were getting ready, taking photos of the process. The girls were starting to fall behind schedule. The bride couldn't find her shoes. They were in the apartment all right, in one of the dozen boxes strewn about the living room. The bride's earrings had been left back at her parent's house. One of the bridesmaids was on the phone, trying to navigate an uncle through the house and direct him to the proper earring box. I think her final words were "just bring all the jewelry you can find." The bride was also having a very hard time getting into her dress; the opening was a bit small for her updo hairstyle.

Suddenly, out of the bedroom where the bride was dressing, we all heard her exclaim, "The NEXT time I get married I'm not doing it like this!" The stunned silence was deafening, thankfully followed by raucous laughter. We all knew she didn't mean it; her exasperation and pre-ceremony jitters had just gotten the best of her. But no, I don't think anyone told her husband that story.

'Maids Worst Nightmare

- Renee Robertson

I was asked to be a bridesmaid by a girl I barely knew. Because her sister lived in another city, I was basically assigned Maid of Honor duties for this nightmare bride.

First, she chose $450 bridesmaids' dresses and was seriously considering asking us to wear Jimmy Choo shoes, which I talked her out of. Then, she asked me to email the wedding party with explicit instructions on how to break in our shoes the week before the wedding. I also had to describe a special undergarment she wanted us to buy so we'd look "shapely" in our dresses. Next came the hair and makeup "timeline," which required us all to meet at the salon at 8 a.m. — for a 6 p.m. wedding ceremony! I think she liked these emails coming from me so she didn't look so crazy.

The final straw was when she wanted my advice on how to tell one bridesmaid she needed to lose weight. She said this girl would "ruin" her pictures at her current weight. I lost it. I told her, "Maybe you should consider being less of a *bitch* so you'll actually have friends after this wedding." And you know what, she didn't ask for my help again until her wedding day!

Unsober Union

- Gina Gallo

I was a guest at a summer wedding at Lake Charles, on a beautiful promontory that jutted out into the water. I got to witness an extremely drunken and fidgety bridal party who snickered and leaned on each other throughout the ceremony. My personal favorite was when the Best Man had to recite his reading from his Blackberry because one of the groomsmen had lost the actual piece of paper. Especially humorous was waiting for each page to load on his phone while he hummed to keep the crowd in suspense.

Adding to the richness of experience, the time that they got married, around 6 p.m., was apparently when the fish in the lake have feeding time. So, intermittently during the ceremony, huge fish were jumping out of the water, into the air, and then splashing very loudly back into the water.

With all this commotion, the bride and groom giggled drunkenly through their vows.

Then, at the reception, they had placed kazoos on all the tables, and every time you blew a kazoo at the happy couple, they had to kiss.

While it was probably the goofiest wedding experience I've had, I loved it. The bride and groom and their wedding party definitely were having fun and not taking the day overly seriously.

Too Many Treats

- Emily Frankovich

Black Diamond is a very special dog. He is the biggest, most handsome Black Lab that you've ever seen. His master, my son-in-law Tom, wanted him to play an important role in his wedding to my daughter, Lydia. The plan was to have the wedding outdoors on a pier under the wide blue skies overlooking Boston Harbor. It was the summer solstice and Father's Day, and we were to have lobster instead of wedding cake. When the festivities were over, the happy couple was going to sail away across the harbor. And Black Diamond was to be the ring bearer.

Well, instead, it rained, poured and blew up quite a storm. We all had to move inside a large tent at the Courageous Sailing Center.

Diamond, who is normally the best-behaved dog in Massachusetts, if not the universe, was upset by all the strangers gathering under the big tent. There was a bagpiper serenading the arriving guests, a sound he had never before heard. There were about a hundred guests, many of whom he had never

met before. Diamond had a temporary guardian, one of the couple's beloved friends, who is not a dog owner. This helpful friend took Diamond on a walk to a grassy lawn near the pier to help him stay relaxed during all the last-minute ceremony preparations.

As the time for the ceremony approached, stress levels everywhere were rising. Diamond felt this too. He woofed his discomfort and was given a dog treat to help calm him down. He woofed again and he got another dog treat, which quieted him for a while until he woofed again. All the while the wind was blowing, the rain was downpouring, and the walls to the tent were billowing.

Then those of us in the front rows heard a strange noise ...

At last, the bridesmaids and ushers made their grand procession and the flower girl sprinkled rose petals on the aisle path. My husband had escorted Lydia in a beautiful long white dress (which was getting soaked with each step) down the aisle to where Tom was waiting for her.

Now it was time for Diamond to shine. At Tom's command he strolled, head high and dignified up the aisle. He delivered the wedding rings in beautiful style. He sat in front of them and seemed happy to obey the command to lie down.

Then those of us in the front rows heard a strange noise.

TOO MANY TREATS

Tom and Lydia suddenly did not have smiling, loving expressions on their faces; they had looks of surprise and shock.

Diamond had upchucked all the doggie treats and grass he had eaten on the floor between the couple. Then he happily laid back down in front of the couple and took a nap.

After a momentary pause, the bride and groom laughed and the ceremony continued. They later described it as a good omen. And thankfully Diamond had missed the shoes of the groom, the officiant and, of course, the bride.

Guest List

Badly Behaved Buddy

- Kelli Schlosser

Although my Big Day was wonderful otherwise, I think my husband's friend made for one of the most obnoxious wedding guests of all time. I had a bad feeling even as we were writing up our guest lists and should have stuck to my guns that this guy not be invited.

My husband has known "Brett" since high school, and I don't think the guy ever really grew up beyond those teenage years. Brett has always been a crazy drinker and partier, wanting to be the center of attention at all costs — even if it means making a fool of himself. He loves when his guy friends retell the stories of his drunken escapades, and every story starts with "one time, Brett got so drunk that …" and ends with, "… and then the security guard threw him out." Needless to say, I was worried about inviting him to our wedding. But my husband insisted that Brett would be hurt if we left him off the guest list, so I finally gave in so long as my husband promised to talk to Brett before the wedding. We even gave Brett a "plus one" in the hopes that he would bring a date who could wrangle him if he started to get out of control.

I was so crazed with wedding planning and making sure every little detail was perfect that I didn't give Brett another thought for the next few months. I literally almost forgot he was coming to the wedding until my new husband and I made our grand entrance into the reception. Brett nearly ran us over on his way to the bathroom; I found out later he had brought his own flask and was making rum and Cokes in the restroom. And there was an open bar!

Things started going downhill when it was time for the toasts. The Best Man is very short and when he stood up to give his speech, Brett shouted from the back of the room "Stand up!" thinking he was being funny. The Best Man turned bright red and fumbled his way through the whole speech because he was so embarrassed. I wanted to strangle Brett.

He took one swig and immediately vomited into the trash can next to the bar.

After two hours of open bar, Brett was dancing up a storm, sliding across the dance floor on his knees, presumably ruining the pants of his rented tux, and practically bowling over our guests in the process. Grandparents were literally jumping out of his way. Then, when it was time for the garter toss, Brett somehow convinced another guest to hoist him up on his shoulders where he drunkenly wobbled all around and yelled for the garter. People are still confused when they see the photos.

The final straw was when the bartender took a break to get more mixers, so Brett decided to go back behind the bar and pour himself a drink. He must have made it a little too strong because he took one swig and immediately vomited into the trash can next to the bar. Livid, I had two groomsman take — or should I say drag — him out of the reception to put him a cab back to his house. Apparently, once outside and waiting for a ride, he proceeded to lie down on the concrete sidewalk in front of the beautiful resort.

At that point, I started to have an "I told you so!" moment with my husband, but then I realized that there was no reason to get upset and let one awful guest ruin the best day of my life. With Brett gone, I put everything else totally out of my mind and had a wonderful rest of the night dancing with my husband and friends.

The redeeming parts? The after-party was so fantastic without Brett (I had been worried that he would be a mess if he made it that far into the night). Better still, it turns out that a friend of mine's father, who worked in the same industry as Brett, had been standing right there when Brett puked in the trash can. After his immature behavior, Brett didn't exactly get offered the summer internship he had wanted from my friend's dad. I definitely felt vindicated.

Wedding Crashers!

- Aaron Hoffman

My fiancée's family really wanted to throw her the wedding of her dreams, so we hired a full-service wedding planner to help us create the event over the course of a year. We decided to host about 150 guests at a very sophisticated and cool hotel in Downtown Los Angeles. Everything about the wedding was lavish, from the 3-foot-tall vases of white orchids to a gourmet candy bar to the Australian lobster tail and filet mignon dinner created by a local celebrity chef. We hosted a cocktail hour before dinner, and my fiancée and I went around greeting all our guests and friends.

Finally, it was time to start seating guests, so I went to find the caterer to let her know that we were about ready to begin serving dinner. As I made my way toward her, I saw her wrapping up plates of food for a well-dressed couple whom I didn't recognize. As they walked away with their "doggie bags," I asked her what was going on. She explained that the two guests said they needed to leave early and wanted to take their dinners to-go. That's when I realized they weren't guests of our wedding — they were wedding crashers!

The caterer must have thought I was nuts, because I immediately ran out the door of the ballroom and in the direction the crashers had gone. I just decided there was no way these two people were going to come uninvited to *my* wedding and get away with it!

I caught up to them near the hotel's lobby, and boy, were they surprised to see the groom chasing after them! As they started jogging towards the parking lot, I shouted to the valet to stop them, that they were crashing my wedding. Two valets jumped out in front of the fake guests and grabbed them.

> The caterer must have thought I was nuts, because I immediately ran out the door ...

When I got up to the couple, I grabbed the wrapped up dinners from the man and his date and said, "Nice try." I felt like James Bond!

The hotel staff escorted the crashers off the property and I went back to our wedding. I immediately found my wife and told her, "You won't believe what just happened!" When I explained to her that I chased down a pair of wedding crashers, she was shocked at first, but then started laughing and said, "Well, at least they didn't get free Surf 'N' Turf!"

Cake Topper Culprit

- Jason Olsen

My girlfriend and I were guests at my high school friend's wedding. The wedding was held in an old ranch-style house that had several rooms of guest tables. When it came time to cut and serve the cake, our table was busy talking and catching up and so it took a bit of time to realize that we had been skipped over by the caterer. My girlfriend said, "Hey, we didn't get cake," and I, wanting to make her happy, said I would go and find us pieces.

The layout of the reception area was a little confusing, and I couldn't track down the caterer. But luckily I walked into a room and there was the cake! I thought, *Jackpot!* As I started cutting out a big slice, I caught a glimpse of someone out of the corner of my eye. I turned and saw the servers all gasping at me with their mouths covered. That's when I realized I had just cut into the couple's cake top that had been set aside to be saved for their first anniversary!

I grabbed the one piece I had already cut, dropped the knife and basically ran out of the room. I was completely panicked thinking,

What if someone else saw me? What if the servers or the caterer rat me out to the groom, a close friend?

I turned and saw the servers all gasping at me with their mouths covered ...

I got back to our table and gave my girlfriend the piece of cake. She was wondering why I didn't get myself one, but I was too freaked out to even explain. I just kept thinking I'd given the couple bad luck in their marriage or, at the very least, ruined their first anniversary.

I guess the servers didn't rat on me, or maybe the caterer devised a way to fix the cake top, but either way, my friend never mentioned the cake top with the missing slice to me. And I never mentioned it to him either.

Streetlamp Exhibitionists

- Katie Beach

Every girl hopes her wedding day will be perfect, and I was no exception to the rule. I accepted the fact that there might be a few mishaps with the day but decided early on that I would accept these snafus and not let them upset me.

My husband and I were planning an outdoor South Carolina wedding for the beginning of August. We checked the weather forecast for two weeks straight. With each check of the weather, we prepared ourselves for the disappointment of having to move our ceremony to an inside location. Luckily, I woke up on our wedding day to a beautiful sky — the sun was shining bright and the temperature was perfect. I remember thinking to myself, "Everything is going to be wonderful; nothing could possibly go wrong!" I was more relaxed than anyone could have imagined.

My brother had become a notary just so he could perform our ceremony. The ceremony was more perfect than anything I could ever have hoped for. There were many laughs and tears of joy shed by all who shared in our day. I was elated that everyone loved the ceremony that I wrote. Because everything had gone so smoothly up to that point, I really thought the rest of the day was going to be just as perfect.

We were getting our pictures taken when the wedding coordinator informed us that we would not be having a wedding cake. Our bakery had "gotten the date wrong" even though they called us at the beginning of the week to confirm all details for the cake that I had designed. Fortunately, the chef was already whipping up a phenomenal dessert for us while our coordinator and DJ called all their contacts to find a "replacement" cake. We decided not to go with a replacement and no one even noticed that we didn't have a cake.

> One of the groomsmen said, "Would you like to see what is happening at your wedding?"

After a bit of disappointment, my husband and I decided we weren't going to let that ruin our day. What we would find out next, however, would.

Fast forward to the reception — dinner was delicious and we were enjoying mingling and dancing with our guests, when one of our groomsman walked up to my husband and me with a camera in his hand. He said, "Would you like to see what is happening at your wedding?" Of course we did. He turned the camera around and *gasp* — there was a picture of two of our guests having sex under a streetlight, right next to where all the guests had parked!

SEX! STREETLIGHT! Really? You're kidding me! I was livid. They could have walked 50 feet to their right and been on a dark secluded golf course, but no.

Children were being held back so they wouldn't see the "action" and other people were snapping pictures left and right. I was utterly embarrassed — mortified even! I was so disappointed and upset that I decided I was done partying at my own wedding. My husband and I had our last dance and wrapped up the reception still in disbelief of what happened.

We left the reception and headed to the airport to catch our flight to Aruba. Upon our arrival home, we received a very sincere apology from the guy partaking in the parking lot action. However, months after the wedding, we still haven't received an apology from the girl. Come to find out, she thinks she did nothing wrong and that if we want an apology we need to go to her. Needless to say, we still haven't spoken to her and I can't help thinking, *Did that really happen?*

In-Laws

A Family Affair

- David White

The days leading up to my wedding took a turn for the really bizarre. This was my second marriage; my first wife had passed away a few years prior. I had two grown daughters with my first wife, both who were attending this wedding.

A few weeks before my wedding, I got a strange phone call from a woman saying she had found my contact information online and needed to speak to me. She was very ominous in her message, although I had no inkling why. When I called her back, imagine my shock when she said, "I wanted to speak to you, because I'm your daughter"!

When my first wife and I had first started dating, she got pregnant. We were very young and just starting out, so we decided to put the baby up for adoption. Apparently, this woman, now 35, had contacted my first wife's family, only to learn that she had passed on. They gave her my name and she found me online. And, she was also living in Seattle! I kept thinking, what if I passed her on the street or in the grocery store and didn't even know it. I was in complete shock, but we agreed to meet at a coffeehouse.

I met with her a few times over the next few weeks. She wanted to see photos of her mother, my first wife, and know more about her. Finally, she wanted to know about her sisters, my two daughters. That's when I realized what I needed to do — invite her to the wedding!

That night, I called my two daughters and told them, "Girls, I never told you because I didn't think I would ever meet her, but you have another sister. She actually lives here in Seattle, and I want to invite her to the wedding." There was total silence on the line. Finally, my oldest daughter, who was helping my fiancée coordinate the wedding, said, "Well, this is crazy ... but I'm sure we can put her at one of the family tables."

> That night, I called my two daughters and told them, "Girls, you have another sister ..."

Next, I had to be sure my bride was OK with inviting this woman to our wedding. She was also fairly shocked. What makes someone curious about their parents after 35 years? But, being the wonderful and compassionate woman that she is, my fiancée said that it wouldn't be right not to include my other daughter in the festivities. After all, it was a celebration of love and family that we wanted to share with everyone.

When I called my daughter to invite her to the wedding,

she was so touched that we both ended up in tears, and I instantly knew I was doing the right thing.

I was a little worried that this would be a distraction on my wedding day, but when the day came, we were so busy and excited that everything was great. My daughters were very sweet to their sister and introduced her to everyone. I think she felt very welcome.

I wasn't sure how people would react, but I knew I wanted to make sure this woman knew she was family and that was accomplished on our wedding day. And it sure makes for a crazy story — the long-lost daughter showing up 6 weeks before my wedding day and meeting her sisters for the first time that day. It sounds like an episode of the *Montell Williams* show!

Like Mother, Like Son

- Angela Wright

I was 19 years old, naive and had never been on my own. A man swept me off my feet and we decided to get married. Unfortunately, I knew very little about his past, his friends, and — my goodness — his family.

On our wedding day, I had to go to my fiancé's house to wake him up because we were just an hour away from having photos taken and he was not answering his phone. Come to find out, the groom and all of his best men were still drunk or hungover from the evening before.

I finally got him in the car, although on our way to get dressed for photos he asked me to pull over approximately 10 times so he could throw up, because he was still so drunk from his bachelor party. I think I should have run then.

I should also mention my parents and my sisters had previously decided they were not coming to the wedding, because they didn't like my fiancé. On the day of the wedding, they called me no less than 50 times to tell me to back out of it, that they would never speak to me again, and remind me that they were not coming to the wedding, which they didn't.

Once we were dressed and had arrived at the venue to have photos taken, all three of my bridesmaids decided, right there at the photo site, that they didn't like the hosiery that I have picked out for them to wear, and they wanted to wear something different. I said no, so they said, it's either our way or the highway. Thus, in my wedding photos, two of my bridesmaids are wearing different colored hosiery than the Maid of Honor. In their short dresses, it looks terrible.

People started arriving, and the ceremony began, but we had no music to walk down the aisle with. Awkwardly, guests started whistling and humming "Here Comes the Bride."

When we arrived at the reception hall, low and behold, my new mother-in-law is stumbling around with vodka in her hand. She had been drinking all day and was so drunk she could barely remember why she was there. The best part of all was she kept going around saying, "I would rather my son be a homosexual than be married to you!"

Good times! That marriage only lasted 13 years.

Funny Shoes

- Andrea Zingerman

I married my husband Igor in August 2009. Although many people would rather ban kids from their wedding and reception, they can be a great source of entertainment!

My husband and I wanted to make our wedding day entertaining for our guests because we like to have fun — this included things having our friend Jack Passion, officially holding the World's Greatest Full Beard title, marry us. But the funniest thing that happened on my wedding day was completely unexpected.

My husband's sister had just given her toast and brought her 4-year-old son up to the table to give us hugs. Apparently the word had reached my nephew that I was wearing funny shoes (they were black 5-inch platform heels and, to his credit, they did look pretty funny) under my dress. He couldn't see them beneath the dress, so he walked up to me, pulled my dress up over his head, (mind you he's about 3 feet tall) yelling, "I want to see the funny shoes!"

Of course, he yelled this in Russian, a language most of our guests did not speak (including me), so we had no idea what he was trying to do! It turned out to be my favorite part of the wedding and an adorable story we'll share for years to come!

Mother Nature Strikes
(And It's Not the Weather)

- Kim Zaharias

Even the best laid plans are no match for Mother Nature. With everything in order for our wedding, I was prepared for going to war with any obstacle that came my way. On our wedding day, the sun was shining and it was going to be a glorious day for sure. My fiancé, Andrew, would be waiting for me at the church along with all of our favorite people. Who cares if the flowers don't show up? I was marrying my best friend.

But if it was such a great day, then why was I suddenly so tired … and cranky … and … oh crap! Cramps! After lots of gleeful "good mornings" from my wedding party, I swigged some OJ and headed for the bathroom. The realization that I had gotten my period was absolutely shocking as I wasn't due to get "it" for another week! Perhaps it was the stress of the wedding.

Sadly, I headed down to tell my future sister-in-law Patty the news about what my wedding night was not going to be. She laughed and said I would too, someday.

After popping some Ibuprofen, the wedding went on, although I had to rush back to the bathroom when we got to the reception hall. Unfortunately, none of my 'maids had done me the honor of toting along a new maxi pad. We went to the hotel's bathroom with giggles, quarters, and a mission. Jen put a quarter in the dispenser and got nothing. Cori headed back to the hall and discretely asked some of the women if they could "give to the cause" and finally found a feminine product. Patty continued to humor me by saying, "I promise you'll laugh about this someday!"

Next problem? My pretty lace underwear with the embroidered hearts were absolutely trashed, along with my hosiery. Cori had a cute new boyfriend and brazenly told us she wouldn't need her underwear for too much longer anyway and offered to donate them! So off we went — me and Patty — to the handicapped stall with Cori's underwear and a new maxi pad in hand while Jen and Cori held the door shut. Patty held my dress high while I sheepishly made the switch.

"It's OK, Kim! Once you've had kids, something like this is really not a big deal," Patty comforted. I had to assume she was telling the truth because she didn't seem fazed by this little adventure.

So I wore someone else's underwear on my wedding day. So my wedding night wasn't quite so exciting. Who cares? My sister-in-law and I laugh — just like she told me we would — every year on my anniversary.

Family Ties

- Robyn Bruns
Red Letter Event Planning
www.redlettereventplanning.com

I met with "Emma" at a local Starbucks to discuss planning her wedding — a black tie event to be held the following New Year's Eve in the Chicago suburbs. Emma and her fiancée had moved out of state but wanted to have the wedding back home. During our conversation Emma explained that she did not get along with her mother "Diane." Looking back, this was quite an understatement.

Emma explained that after her engagement she called her dad at work to announce the happy news and told him to the pass on the information to her mom if he wanted, she didn't care either way. Emma was quite pleased with this lack of correspondence and further explained to me that if she could get away with not inviting her mother to the wedding she would have no qualms about it. However, she did want her dad there and he would not attend if Diane was not invited.

As a professional wedding consultant I had run into my share of Mothers of the Bride. I assured Emma that I would be able to handle her mom and that part of my role as her wedding planner would be as a neutral third party. My experience has been that brides may disparage their mothers from time to time but, in the end, there is a loving relationship. In Emma's case I had no idea I was about to witness the worst mother-daughter dysfunction I have ever seen or probably will ever see as a wedding consultant.

Even though Emma had forewarned me about her feelings for her mother I was really taken aback the first time she referred to a family friend as her "good" mom and her real mother as her "bad" mom. The "good" mom helped her pick out her wedding dress and went to the catering tasting. "Bad" mom was not invited to participate in these or any other wedding activities.

I was about to witness the worst mother-daughter dysfunction I will probably ever see.

Communication is a big part of my job, and it isn't unusual for me to have meetings or calls with parents of my clients. The bride and groom usually participate, however. In this case, I was the only one who communicated with Diane about guest lists, wedding details, etc. Emma continued her boycott of communication with Diane throughout the whole year or more of wedding planning.

When we met with vendors, one of the first things Emma would tell them was that she did not get along with her mom. Emma asked the photographer not to take any pictures if Diane was standing right next to her and insisted there be a buffer zone of one or two people in any shot with Diane.

She told the videographer that in the final video she did not want to see or hear her mom. She helpfully suggested that when shooting the raw footage if they just ignored her mom it would be easier to accomplish this in the final cut.

Emma also told me that she had assigned a friend's mom duties. This person's job during the wedding was to keep Diane away from her, preferably out of her field of vision throughout the whole wedding day.

The ultimate "I don't get along with my mom" moment happened two weeks before the planned New Year's Eve extravaganza. The bride and groom flew to Hawaii and got married in a beachfront ceremony with the "good" mom in attendance! Emma was determined that her mother not be present because, in her mind, the only way to have a happy wedding day would be if Diane was not there.

The elegant $80,000 black tie celebration that occurred two weeks later that Diane attended was not the couple's real wedding and only a few close friends (and her wedding consultant) knew the truth that, indeed, Emma had not invited her mom to her wedding after all.

Guest of Honor

- Keith Jagdhuber
Antrim 1844 Country House Hotel
www.antrim1844.com

Several years ago, I had clients for a May wedding. The day before the big event we had made arrangements for the groom's family to bring us all of their personal belongings. As we unloaded their SUV, I noticed a blue and white ginger jar and asked if that too was for the reception.
In unison, the siblings both exclaimed, "Yes, we brought Dad!" You got it, the groom's father had passed away and his cremated remains were in the ginger jar.

I was given explicit directions to place Dad on the mantle in the ballroom for the reception so he too could be with us for the wedding day, and to not mention it to anyone.

I followed their instructions. I kept Dad in my office for the night, and the morning of the Big Day I placed him carefully on the mantle in the ballroom.

The wedding was gorgeous. Flawless and tasteful. Toward the end of the evening, I directed my staff to start to collect the personal belongings. I gave explicit directions not to touch the ginger jar on the mantle.

Well, sometimes staffers do not listen. To my dismay, I watched one of my long-time employees get the jar off the mantle. I tried to run in her direction but was sidetracked by the bride with a question. Now, this particular employee is, shall I say, nosey! I watched her as she came across the ballroom holding the jar carefully, but at the same time taking off the lid and, yes, sticking her hand in the jar.

> I gave explicit directions not to touch the ginger jar on the mantle. Well, sometimes staffers do not listen.

I made eye contact with her at the same moment she realized what was in the jar. When the bride had left, we laughed hysterically, never told anyone, and packed up Dad without any further incident.

Monster in Law

- Anonymous

Have you ever wondered why some of us have become wedding planners?

I met my Prince Charming in 2001, at a Halloween party, and we clicked instantly. His mother, however, was not the most welcoming. I think she thought the relationship wouldn't last.

Three and a half years later, he proposed and the wedding nightmare began. I wanted to get married in October, his mother said February. So February it was. Luckily, I had already picked out my wedding gown and attendants, because those are the only things I had the pleasure of choosing. The venue, church, wedding colors, music, cake, flowers, food, pastor — everything was picked by his mother. My mother was not even allowed to help at all.

The wedding day came and we felt like just going to Vegas and having Elvis marry us at that point, but we stuck it out. I was a non-emotional bride by that point. We ran through our vows but got held up by the photographer at the church for two hours!

When we got to the reception, half our guests had already left. We danced a little and tried to enjoy ourselves. By the end of the night, we left hungry (we didn't get any food at the reception, by the way), tired, and my new hubby was a bit tipsy, so we went to bed.

My wedding experience is why I became a wedding planner. I want everyone else to avoid a day such as mine. I want people to have a truly magical experience.

> We felt like just going to Vegas and having Elvis marry us at that point ...

I should say this story ends on a happy note. I am still married to my Prince, we now have a Princess, and my mother-in-law has since apologized for her mistakes.

All Choked Up

- Crista Tharp
Tharp Events
www.tharpevents.com

I had a wedding a few years ago where the Mother of the Bride was a very strong personality. This is always a bit difficult to deal with because you want to be respectful yet protect your bride at the same time. This mom was adamant about several details on the wedding day — most of them things I advise against. But at her insistence, the 2-year-old ring bearer had the actual rings on his pillow.

I can still see it so vividly in my mind. We were all lined up in the back getting ready for the procession into the church. I was across the room helping a guest and I looked at Sam (his name is changed to protect the guilty) as he was untying the rings. As I crossed the room quickly he put his hand, which held the rings, up to his mouth. By this time, the bridesmaids and others in the line saw what was happening. All at once about 12 people were loudly whispering, "Sam! Sam!" This must have scared him so much that he actually swallowed the rings.

Luckily, there was a guest who was a doctor and Sam was just fine. The rings however, would not be available for the ceremony. Instead, we had two guests offer up their rings for the nuptials and all was well.

The moral of this story: Listen to your wedding planner!

Ceremony

Call of the Wild

- Glenna Tooman
  Memory Makers Event Planning
  www.memorable-events.com

I live and work in Southwestern Idaho and Eastern Oregon. Many of our weddings occur in outdoor settings, often in rural areas where wildlife and weather can present challenges. In 2002, I had a wedding at a winery located about 40 miles from Boise. The temperature that day was 110 degrees. It was one of the hottest summers on record. The first mishap occurred about 5 miles from the winery where I encountered road construction. With gravel flying up from cars going by, I rolled up the windows and sat in the sweltering car while I called the cake baker, florist, and DJ to let them know they needed to plan on delays.

As we prepared for the ceremony, brief rain showers kept brewing over the nearby Snake River. It would rain for maybe 30 seconds, and the storm would move on. That happened four or five times, just long enough to hide the guest book, then bring it out again. We finally started the ceremony, with the bride entering to lightning in the distance.

During the ceremony, a bull snake decided to join us (wineries love snakes because they keep the rodent population in check). The snake wiggled its way through the seated guests and headed for the bride and groom. One of the guests leaped from her chair, then caught the attention of an usher who was standing in the back. He walked over, picked up the snake, which was about three and a half feet long, then posed for a photo before carrying it to the hillside and tossing it into the apple orchards below.

> The snake wiggled its way through the seated guests and headed for the bride and groom.

I talked with the bride several weeks after the wedding. She mentioned that she had seen their uninvited guest as the usher walked behind the groom with the snake. She said they had so many special memories from their day and the little mishaps added an extra touch to the day.

At another wedding the following year, we were joined by muskrats. The wedding was held at an amphitheater on a small lake. The wedding party stood on a platform built over the water. During the ceremony, two muskrats came out of the lake and chased each other around the platform, totally oblivious to the humans standing there. Fortunately, they decided to leave before the wedding party exited.

When we do back-country weddings, we have to be careful with food, dirty dishes, and anything else that might attract bears, raccoons and other wildlife. Forest Service personnel usually drive by to check our permits and to provide instruction on what to do in case of unwanted visitors. Their instructions generally include bringing large pots and pans to bang together to create noise that will scare the critters away. At one wedding, however, the guests were not wild, but rather cattle that had gotten loose. We had to pick up their "deposits" before the guests arrived.

I love my job and the opportunities it provides to create memorable weddings and events in settings that have special meaning to the bride and groom, including any errant wildlife that might decide to join us.

Fire of Fertility

- Crystal Lequang
  Amazáe Special Events
  www.amazaespecialevents.com

It started off as a beautiful ceremony and ended with an unbelievable, memorable event that was nearly a huge disaster. I wish we could say we didn't know it was coming.

We were all ready for a perfect Eastern Indian wedding ceremony to take place at the beautiful Sofitel in Redwood City, California. Rupa and Rudy were a great couple and they really wanted their guests to experience their Indian traditions, food and culture, as well as have the modernization of Western etiquette. They did a great job balancing these two with meal options that included the wonderful French-influenced food at the Sofitel as well as contracting them to include an Indian entrée option. They were fully attired in Indian outfits, but groomsmen wore traditional tuxes. They had a traditional cake but had a fabulous statue topper of an Indian couple in the exact attire they were in. A great balance between the worlds.

In traditional Hindu ceremonies like this one the priest also serves as an MC for the ceremony. The priest in this ceremony was extremely adamant that the wedding coordinators stay out of his way. He kept insisting that he had been doing this for years, and he did not need the assistance of anyone. We honored his wishes and let him do things his way but, of course, we were on full alert.

As a central part of traditional Hindu ceremonies, the couple goes through a series of symbolic gestures. One of these gestures includes walking seven times around a pit of fire, while saying seven vows to each other. The fire represents a force greater than man, a Radiant One.

The fire grew to a wall of about 3 feet and people began to shift their collars and remove layers of clothing.

During the ceremony, the priest kept adding more fuel to the fire. The fuel consisted of different food items, such as clarified butter, puffed rice and yogurt, being placed into the fire. All these items are said to bring richness and fertility to the couple. As the priest talked, he kept adding more items to the fire and it grew, and grew, and grew. The air in the ballroom started heating up as the fire grew to an unmanageable wall of about 3 feet and people began to shift their collars and remove layers of clothing.

Against the advice of others, the priest continued to add more to the fire, which caused the fire to continue to grow.

He was still adamant that he had been doing this for years and didn't need anyone's help. Next thing we knew, the fire was huge and almost ceiling high — a ceiling that just been repainted 2 months ago, unfortunately. Everyone hustled to open the doors out of fear that the fire alarm would go off. Others were looking for the fire extinguisher, and we were making preparations to evacuate folks.

Miraculously, somehow, the fire ended up being contained. At this point, we weren't sure if the laughter in the room was out of true happiness or nervousness. Although on the verge of disaster, it managed to be a very memorable event. In fact, the couple had contracted for a same-day video recap of the ceremony service to be shown at the reception, and everyone had good laugh when we relived the moment again.

It is safe to say that this couple's ceremony and reception were very memorable, and the fertility fire must have worked, as Rupa had a baby very soon after!

Celebrity Sighting

- Loren Scott
  Loren Scott Photography
  www.LorenScottPhotography.com

I was photographing a wedding at a large Catholic church in Los Angeles a few years ago. For some reason, the bride decided to have her dress delivered to the church the day of the wedding. The dress tailor finally arrived with the dress 45 minutes after the ceremony was supposed to begin. Again, this was a Catholic church where weddings are usually an hour or so long and they rush you right out immediately after the ceremony to make room for confessionals, the next wedding, or whatever else they have packed into the day's schedule.

As the tailor and bridesmaids were helping the bride get into the dress, the bride asked about "the rest of the dress." There was also supposed to be a 6-foot train attached to the back of the dress. The tailor started explaining that there had been "an accident." I heard the bride yell, "What accident?" After the tailor explained that she had cut her finger while doing some stitching on the train, getting a small blood stain on it, so she just did not bring it, the bride went nuts. She stormed into the adjoining room, slammed the door behind her, and started screaming and beating on the walls.

This lasted about 60 seconds, but seemed like an eternity. When she came back out, she said, "Let's just get this over with." Everyone tried to assure her that the dress looked just beautiful as it was, which it really did.

The church coordinator rushed us out, the ceremony started, and they blasted through it in about 15 minutes — perhaps a record for a formal Catholic wedding.

Then, we went off to the Los Angeles Biltmore for the reception. I saw Jesse Jackson and his entourage walking through the lobby and discovered that his birthday bash was happening in the ballroom next to our event. Everything at the wedding seemed to be going well and back to normal when we went up to the balcony to photograph the cake and the happy couple cutting it.

When they saw the cake, they got quiet for a moment and finally said, "This is not our cake. Our cake was a three-tiered square white cake." The cake in front of them was a three-tiered round chocolate cake with a monogrammed "J" on the side of it. A "J," as in "Jesse Jackson."

The bride asked me if we could Photoshop out the "J" on the cake, and when I confirmed that we certainly could, she said, "We're cutting this cake!" which they promptly did. My guess is that, in the next ballroom, Jesse Jackson was wondering why his birthday cake looked a lot like a wedding cake.

Communion No-No

- Merry Miller
  www.HarpMusicToGo.com

In this case, I was the one who caused an extremely embarrassing scene at a wedding! A friend asked me to attend a wedding with him in the Hamptons. I had met the bride and groom at their engagement party and developed a huge crush on the Best Man.

The wedding was extremely upscale, with about 400 guests, and the ceremony was held in a beautiful Catholic church. I am Protestant, not Catholic, but decided to partake in communion in order to smile at the Best Man. Horrible idea — but I was 23 years old and had a crush.

So I walked to the front of the church and smiled and winked at the Best Man as the priest put the sacrament in my hand. Instead of immediately putting it in my mouth — because I had never taken Catholic communion — I walked back to my row. Suddenly, I heard the priest scream, "YOU WALKED AWAY WITH THE BODY OF CHRIST!" He actually left the pulpit and ran to my row!

Everyone in the church looked at me — I was beyond mortified. I shoved the wafer in my mouth and just sat down.

The entire night at the reception, everyone who saw me remarked, "Hey you're the chick who took the body of Christ," and laughed.

> Suddenly, I heard the priest scream ...

Alas, there were no fireworks between the Best Man and me. I learned that he only dated Jewish girls, so that eliminated me — especially since I am named after the Christmas holiday! Instead, I ended up dating my friend who took me as his date to the wedding for the next year, and we are still good friends today. And even years later, this embarrassing story still comes up!

Scuba Wedding

- Maryann & Michael Cambrick

We had a very wet wedding — and I don't mean that it rained! Michael and I met seven years ago in a scuba training class and had taken several diving trips together while we were dating. From night diving with giant manta rays to exploring abandoned shipwrecks in the Bahamas, scuba is an important aspect of our history together.

I can't say our families were very happy when we decided to have an underwater wedding off the coast of Fort Lauderdale. No one else in our family is scuba certified, which means they couldn't join us underwater for the ceremony. You wouldn't believe how many people told us we were being stubborn and even selfish, but we maintained that getting married underwater was our dream!

First, we booked a boat that had glass panels along the bottom so our 60 guests could watch the ceremony. Then, we invited 4 of our friends who we often take dive trips with to be our underwater witnesses. On the day of the wedding, we were also equipped with Ocean

Technology Systems masks, which allowed us to talk to each other underwater. We could speak our vows, and the sound was streamed up to the boat so our guests could listen, too. There was also a streaming video they could watch at the same time.

I'll admit it was a bit of a wild, out-there wedding ceremony, and some guests got a little seasick up on the boat, but we were in perfect happiness beneath the waves. We were able to exchange vows and have an underwater kiss, with all our loved ones looking on in one way or another.

> We had a very wet wedding — and I don't mean that it rained!

Once we got back on dry land, we changed into our dancing shoes and had a traditional reception at the beach club. Over tropical drinks and a large fire pit, the same guests who were concerned that we were having such a "bizarre" ceremony commented on how special, personal and unique the underwater wedding was.

You should see the looks on people's faces when we tell them how and where we got married, but we wouldn't really have it any other way!

And for our honeymoon, can you guess what we did?

Loving Memory Burning Bright

- Cathy Brim
  Bloom Floral Design
  www.bloomfloraldesign.biz

Let me tell you about one wedding that gave everyone goosebumps. I am a florist and booked a wedding for two lovely individuals, Dena and Thomas. The ceremony and reception were to be held at the home of the groom, which was situated on a small lake in a neighborhood of Atlanta.

The ceremony itself took place on the banks of the lake, in front of a small inlet. Dena and Thomas had set up an arch for the backdrop of their vows. They had asked me for some ideas on doing a "memorial candle" in honor of Thomas's father who had passed away recently. I suggested wrapping a Styrofoam wreath with ribbon and placing a bubble bowl in the center of the wreath with a pillar candle inside.

Thomas rigged up a little pulley across the inlet so that the wreath and candle could float in the perfect center of the water.

The ceremony was beautiful and after Dena and Thomas said their vows, they lit the memorial candle, attached it to pulley and floated it out.

The evening continued with a sweet reception in the backyard. I had lined the wall that edged the lake with bubble bowls and candles to complement the memorial candle and add sparkle to the lakewater. However, a storm was on its way and it started to get quite windy. All the candles went out before the reception was over. The reception ended just in time as the storm blew in and it rained all night.

The groom's mother told me there was something I had to see ...

I had to return to the wedding site the next day to pick up some things, and the groom's mother met me at the door. She told me there was something I had to see. We walked through the backyard, which was littered with sticks, branches and leaves from the storm the night before. We got down to the edge of the lake, and there, floating in the perfect middle of the water was the memorial candle, its flame still burning bright.

Hurricane Frances Comes to Town

- Angela Doyle

My boyfriend was Best Man in a wedding being held in Vero Beach, Florida. We were booked in a beautiful hotel, next to the oceanfront venue where the wedding ceremony and reception were being held. Three weeks before the October wedding, I was reading the news online when I saw a photo of a town that had been completely ravaged by Hurricane Frances — it was Vero Beach.

Shortly thereafter, we were notified by the bride and groom that everyone's accommodations were being changed because the first resort had been hit hard by the hurricane. I'll never forget my boyfriend's face when he looked up from the couple's email and asked, "What's Dodgertown?"

Fast-forward to the wedding weekend, when my boyfriend and I arrived at Dodgertown, which was, in fact, a shabby one-story motel next to the soggy baseball fields where the Los Angeles Dodgers held Spring Training. However, the drive from the airport reinforced the fact that there were *no* other hotels in the area that hadn't been thrashed by Hurricane Frances. Other hotels had bathrooms exposed where brick walls had literally peeled away in the wind. Dodgertown was one of the only places left unscathed, but no wonder it was the bride's last resort — there was tacky Dodgers decor everywhere and everything was damp, mildewy and muddy. At the small cocktail party the couple had that night in their room, the bride apologized ten times for the lack of sophistication. I mostly felt bad for *her*.

But that didn't compare to the ceremony site. When we got to the wedding, we gasped at the driftwood, trash, and murky, smelly sludge that had washed up on the beach after the storm. What had once been a beautiful beach beside which to have a wedding ceremony was now a rotting dump. Obviously there had been no place to relocate the wedding on such short notice, so the bride just moved the ceremony beside the hotel's pool. Even with the beach now 30 feet away, it was a bad sight. Everything was cracked and damaged. Wood siding had ripped off and windows were broken and boarded up. The bride was visibly upset as she walked down the aisle and the wind — leftover from the hurricane — blasted us throughout the ceremony.

Thankfully, the reception moved us inside where the ballroom was cozy and distracted everyone from the gray skies, stinking beach and post-hurricane destruction. The bride tried to enjoy herself and, in the end, it was a nice wedding — memorable for more reasons than one. My boyfriend (now-fiancé!) and I still joke we're going to honeymoon at Dodgertown.

Marriage Misnomer

- Kristie Koehn
  Pampered Passions Fine Lingerie
  www.pamperedpassions.com

My husband Dennis and I were married in May 2007. We had an outdoor ceremony with a wedding arch and beautiful gerbera daisies decorating it. Before the wedding even started, a huge gust of wind blew the arch away, along with all of the flowers on it.

Despite my disappointment, the wedding started and all seemed to be going as planned. That is, until the minister said, "Kristie and Bruce are joined today ..." Remember, my husband's name is Dennis. I leaned in and replied, "This is Dennis ... he doesn't know about Bruce." The entire crowd burst out laughing and Dennis was known as "Bruce" for the rest of the evening!

In the aftermath of my wedding day, I was told about another crazy thing that occurred that evening. A dear friend of mine who, in her mid-40s, had just endured a nasty divorce after 18 years of marriage, attended with a date. At one point during the reception, a line formed for the first floor bathroom (our venue was an old manor with only three bathrooms and the guests did not know about the other two bathrooms upstairs). Turns out my friend and her date were having "relations" in the first floor bathroom, hence the hold up!

All ended well, however, as my friend and her date ended up getting married!

Ceremony Gone Batty

- Rev. Chris Mohr
Foothills Chapel
www.foothillschapel.com

As an officiant, I've seen some pretty outrageous things happen during weddings, like the time the nervous 16-year-old sister of the bride was supposed to hit the CD button on the boombox for the processional music and she hit the Tuner button instead. The Carly Simon song "You're No Good" poured out of the speakers. The guests were mortified at first, but when the bride laughed, everyone else laughed along with her and it made for a great story.

About 15 years ago, though, I encountered a bride with less of a sense of humor. She was having a backyard wedding, and her parents had already spent tens of thousands of dollars to re-landscape their lawn and garden. The whole area was decorated to the nines, with dozens of large flower arrangements, multiple archways, marble pillars and much more. For the comfort of the guests there were electronic mosquito and bug "zappers" up on poles at strategic locations. It seemed that the bride had thought of everything, and she wanted nothing less than a wedding that was absolutely perfect in every detail.

The bride had decided to go on a crash diet about six weeks before her wedding and had managed to lose a lot of weight. It seems she had skipped the re-fitting, so I was worried the dress might literally fall off of her when she walked down the aisle.

The string quartet began to play the processional and, as the last bridesmaid walked into her place, I heard a strange electronic buzzing sound, the kind of sound you'd hear in a mad scientist's laboratory. I looked over my left shoulder and to my horror I saw that a bat had flown into the bug zapper just behind me. Its wings were fully outstretched, its face contorted, and its whole body was on fire. An eerie fluorescent light was traveling up and down the zapper. It was a vision from "that place" I try to keep all my parishioners from ever going.

> The bride looked at me with an expression that said, "Just *do* the ceremony."

As the bride walked down the aisle, gasps of horror gave way to stifled giggles. But this bride did not think the burning bat was at all funny. Following her lead, I kept a straight face. When she walked up to the front, the crowd was almost out of control. Then, just after her father gave her away, both of her garters fell down her newly slimmed legs and were dangling on her ankles. The crowd's laughter could no longer be contained. The bride looked at me with an expression that said, "Please don't you laugh too — just *do* the ceremony." Using all my discipline, without once cracking a smile, I performed the ceremony with gravitas.

Usually when something goes a little wrong at a ceremony, I make light of it with a brief comment and let the crowd laugh a bit, then get right back to performing a ceremony that is completely heartfelt and sincere. It's a way of saying, "Don't sweat the small stuff." This time, however, there was no room for making light of it!

Thankfully, other than the burning bat and the dangling garters, everything went beautifully at that wedding.

Rambling Reverend

- Lisa Muir

A few years ago, I attended my now-fiancé's brother's wedding. Let me start by saying that this couple is late to everything. In fact, we all were certain that the bride would be late to her own wedding.

The wedding was taking place in a banquet hall, the same room as the reception. All of the guests were seated at their tables. Sure enough, the wedding started a whole 90 minutes after the original start time. While we waited there was no music, no appetizers, no drinks — nothing. An hour and a half later, the music finally started to play and the bride walked down the aisle.

Then the preacher started in and we were just relieved that the wedding was underway. Except that he went on and on and on for an hour! He spoke about everything except the couple. He kept saying, "When the well runs 'dry ..." I have no idea what he was talking about, as I'm sure none of the other guests did either. All the guests were sighing, rolling their eyes, and snickering. I felt so bad for the bride. Here it was, her wedding day, and it was ruined.

Finally the preacher married the couple — but only because the groom stepped in and said, "OK, enough already, let's finish!"

Guests were sighing, rolling their eyes, and snickering ...

Dinner was served quickly. Everything ended up having to be rushed, because the couple only had the hall for a certain amount of time. There was literally no music and certainly no time for dancing or celebrating. The worst part was, it turns out that the couple was late because their baby daughter had been in the ER overnight with an asthma attack!

Now that my fiancé and I are getting married, he jokes that he's going to get the same officiant to marry us. And I say, "Over my dead body! Unless of course you want the well to run dry!"

Reception

Complete Cruise Catastrophe

- Jennifer & Michael Cabuay

I have been blessed with finding a soulmate and lifetime partner in Michael. Michael and I are in our thirties — a more mature bride and groom with little want for a large wedding — so we went searching for more informal wedding ideas. If he had the choice we would have eloped and, in retrospect, we probably should have!

With my goal being to find a venue and atmosphere that would keep things casual and cost-effective, I set out on my research. In Michael and my discussions relating to honeymoons an idea for a cruise presented itself. The lightbulbs went off! Norfolk, Virginia Port is only 20 minutes away and has four or five cruise lines departing from there. We found a cruise line that would be able to accommodate a wedding onboard while docked in Norfolk. We briefly discussed how they would accommodate a small wedding in a cozy venue like the library. The wedding coordinator's vision was right on target with what I was looking for.

So April 10 became our wedding date. We also planned to take the cruise's 11-day trip to the Caribbean after the wedding, as our honeymoon.

I booked the cruise, signed the coordinator contract and enjoyed the holidays.

Maybe I was getting too confident that things had fallen into place. The seventh dress I tried on off-rack at a Richmond bridal store was "the dress." It needed only slight adjustments and cost — imagine — under $500. This is a breeze, I thought; the only thing I had left to do was make a few fun decisions about the cake, food and flowers, and get the marriage license. All these arrangements were completed in four months, no sweat.

Having all this extra time, I organized a timeline, arranged elaborate guest welcome baskets, printed up invitations to the welcome dinner, planned an outing for the girls, compiled a photographer checklist, made a limousine schedule, and even pre-purchased an excursion for the honeymoon. I booked horseback riding in the Bahamas port — something we both really wanted to do. With all this organization, what could possible go wrong?

Two days before my Sunday-afternoon wedding, I got a call from the wedding coordinator; she had just heard the ship was to be delayed coming into port, delaying the ceremony by an hour. This was not good news, as we had guests flying out that night. Of course, the arrival of the ship was beyond anyone's control, so she planned to keep me informed of any additional news. I notified the groom, guests and limousine service of the changes and went on with our evening. But I admit I lost sleep, not able to shake the feeling there would be more unwelcome adjustments.

Saturday, I received a call from my father who had seen a small article in the paper that said the expected arrival of the ship would not be until 3 p.m., delaying the ceremony again. Slightly frazzled, I left a message for the wedding coordinator and went on with our planned girls outing to the spa for manicures and pedicures. I thought, *All I know at this point is that I am getting married tomorrow, one way or another.* But the stress was starting to show.

That evening, all the out of town guests met at the welcome dinner. It was a nice evening, good food, great company, with much bonding and warmth. My father gave a speech welcoming his son-in-law to the family and jokingly wishing us "that your ship may come in."

> If he had the choice we would have eloped and, in retrospect, we probably should have!

Sunday, I was leisurely taking my time getting ready and enjoying the morning, when the coordinator called again. The ship would not be able to be boarded until later and she had to move the ceremony to the Marriott in town in order to accommodate anyone flying out in the early evening. She said we would have a champagne toast and then proceed to the ship for the reception afterward. I really had no say at this point. I contacted my groom, the guests and the limo, and wrote a "revised revised" timeline.

The limousine picked us up on time and we proceeded

to the hotel. We were hurried up to the third floor where we were shown to a small hospitality suite set up with chairs. The coordinator then informed me that there was no photographer because he was on the ship. So much for the photographer's checklist! Luckily, I did bring half a dozen disposable cameras, so we put them out on chairs for guests to use.

I was feeling a bit frazzled — the room was not what I had in mind for the ceremony, and I was not pleased that there was no photographer. But, I was getting married and I was determined that nothing was going to ruin the day. I put on my gown and tiara and spent a few girly moments with my sister, my mom and my friend. I walked into the room glowing, seeing my nervous groom awaiting my arrival. We took our vows, lit candles, exchanged rings, and gave each other a great big kiss. We were married — a big sigh of relief (or so we thought)!

The remaining guests who were not departing for the airport were then rushed aboard the ship to the reception area called the Crow's Nest. I smiled to see the sign saying "Reserved for Michael and Jennifer's Wedding," then frowned to see the room was filled with cruise passengers waiting to depart. Nothing was set up or waiting for us. To make matters worse, the Crow's Nest is a bar with neon lights. We had discussed the library, so how had it come to a disco bar? I was at a loss for how to keep the reception going on a pleasant note. Luckily, my mother could read the distress on my face. She had the coordinator show her alternative venues and we were moved to a smaller, cozier

Piano Bar, which was a little more sophisticated and a better fit for the wedding group.

Again, nothing was organized and nothing seemed to go right. Only after I put in my own CD did we get a First Dance, and only after our guests rearranged the furniture. Some guests complained of dirty lavatories. The photographer was rather disgruntled and wanted to parade our worn-out and hungry guests around the boat for pictures. I replied, "Not a chance; do what you can here."

Finally, cold hors d'oeuvres arrived, to a ravenous reception. Though our wedding group was offered a meal at the Pinnacle Grill, the nicest restaurant on the cruise, our guests were exhausted from the hurry-up-and-wait progression of day and just wanted to leave. I then cried my first tears of disappointment while apologizing to my supportive and wonderful wedding guests.

My husband and I, now alone, tried to encourage each other back to a more optimistic attitude, as we had an 11-day cruise and one exciting excursion on horseback ahead of us. We went to the front desk for keys and then to our room, which was not upgraded by the cruise line to make up for our inconvenience, as had been suggested. At least our luggage was there. Being rather tired we stayed in our wedding attire and went to eat in the main dining room, being stared at like lunatics. But who cares, the worst was over — or so we hoped.

Upon returning to our cabin, we found a note under our door that said the ship, still under repair, was required to skip the Bahamas port, and we would be refunded the port charges of $13.22 per person. That also meant we would miss our horseback riding — the only excursion we booked! What next?!

The next day, we woke to voices right on the other side of our window, and we realized we were on the ship level and any Peeping Tom could have peeked right in! Finally, we were upgraded to the verandah deck, although we could barely relax because Michael was so seasick.

We signed up for a few mediocre excursions in different ports and tried to enjoy ourselves. At one point, we were excited to be going to San Juan, but no, due to the fact that the ship was still in disrepair, we had to skip Puerto Rico and return straight to our originating port. They refunded us the port charges and gave us 20 percent off our next cruise fare. *Who would come back after all this?* I wondered.

> The photographer wanted to parade our worn-out guests around the boat for pictures. I replied, "Not a chance."

The second port cancellation was the last disappointment I could take, and I wept uncontrollably that evening. I had put all the hopes and dreams of my important wedding day and honeymoon with this cruise line — in the little ship that couldn't. While feeling like a trapped animal on the rolling, dragging ship I, for the first time in my life, got seasick. We were grateful for the upgraded room because we ended up spending quite some time in it.

After three more days at sea, the boat pulled into our originating port. We were so glad to be off that ship. But it didn't end there. When Michael went to get copies of our marriage license in order to process my name change, the court had no record of receiving it! So after all that, we were not even legally married! Thank goodness we had a bunch of pictures, courtesy of our guests, to prove we did sign it.

Finally, one last drama: 72 hours after returning from the cruise, both my husband and I were taken sick with 102-degree temperatures! Anyone else agree that we should have eloped?

Smoke Out

- Ray Zajeski
  The Connexion Band
  www.connexionband.com

My band has been performing in the Chicago area for the past 30 years. One of my favorite wedding tales is when all the guests at the reception were seated in a large, beautiful tent for the dinner service. Since it was windy, the sides were zip-tied closed to keep the cool Chicago air out. All the tables and chairs were draped with expensive white linens and the floral arrangements were outstanding. It was a classy, beautiful event.

We started to introduce the wedding party into the tent and everything was going perfectly until there was a last-minute plan for each guest to light an oversized sparkler for the bride and groom's introduction. All the guests stood up, cheering and holding their lit sparklers.

At first, it was exciting and beautiful ... and then came the smoke. The sparkler smoke quickly filled the tent to the point that no one could see in front of them! The guests did not know how to extinguish the sparklers, so some started to pour their water and bar drinks over the sparklers. Some guests even began to dip them into the flower vases. Panic broke out and everyone was rushing for the only exit out of the tent, coughing from the smoke.

After the sides of the tent were cut open and all of the smoke cleared, the reception looked like a total wreck. There were dark burn marks on the table linens, napkins, flowers and vases, and splattered water all over the tables. Thankfully, no one was injured, but I'm sure everyone will remember the sparkler wedding.

All's Well That Ends Well

- Theresa Minnette
Theresa Minnette Photography
www.theresaminnette.com

It was a beautiful day for a wedding at one of the nicest venues nestled in the wine valley of Temecula, California. Every detail had been professionally and perfectly planned, and love was in the air. As the photographer, I was the first vendor to arrive so I could get my equipment arranged and begin capturing the day as it unfolded. However, I'd never captured a day quite like this one before!

As the bride arrived, everything seemed in order. Her gorgeous dress hung in the window and bridesmaids patiently waited for mirror time as the bride's makeup and hair artists went to work. A knock at the door revealed the wedding planner. A very concerned look had replaced her usual smile as she informed our bride that the wedding cake vendor had just been involved in an automobile accident. Thankfully, no one was seriously injured, but the cake exploded like a grenade, speckling the inside of the car with icing. The bride kept her composure and immediately called her mom to run by the nearest grocery store to grab a cake.

Once everyone was dressed, we began taking

shots of the bride and her bridesmaids. A couple of early guests milled about as vendors scurried with last-minute preparations. The florist was decorating the landscape and altar with beautiful lilies, which really impressed the bride, since she didn't pay for any lilies. It wasn't until the florist delivered the bride her bouquet and corsages that the bride's own smile faded to a look of concern. "Whose bouquet is this?" she asked. After a few awkward minutes of discussion, the florist realized she'd delivered the wrong order! Her company had two weddings that day and had crossed their delivery! "Well, at least I have flowers," the bride said, optimistically.

By this time, the seats had filled with guests and the music from the string quartet signaled the song prior to the Wedding March. It was time! Everyone took their spots, and the mothers of the bride and groom joined one another at the altar, each with a glass vase of colored sand that would be mixed into a single container by the bride and groom to represent the coming together of the two families.

As the ladies returned to their seats and the groomsmen took their places, the sound of shattering glass was a stark contrast to the beautiful music of the quartet. You could hear the low rumble of "Awwws" as hands covered mouths in the crowd. Either the wind or one of the groomsmen (depending on whom you ask) knocked over the vases of sand and sent them crashing to the concrete floor. I saw a slight tear in the bride's eye, but she smiled and said, "Well, that's one way to mix the sand!"

The ceremony itself went well, and the couple was brought together in holy matrimony, through good times and bad. This should have been an omen that the bad times were not quite over for the day!

The reception was a wonderful meal of filet mignon topped with balsamic syrup and goat cheese, King Crab leg, braised potatoes and asparagus tips in garlic butter. The string quartet continued to entertain while the guests were served, but I could tell by the disgruntled look on the wedding coordinator's face that something wasn't quite right.

I went over to see if I could help her with anything. She was falling to pieces at this point because she had to go tell the bride and groom that the caterers dropped a container with 16 plates of food, and they had to pick which two tables of guests wouldn't be served! Before I could even offer my condolences, the wedding coordinator, overcome by stress, fell to the floor and began convulsing! She was anemic and was having a seizure right on the lawn next to the wedding dining area!

I felt so bad for the bride and groom. They'd put so much into making their wedding perfect, but an unfortunate sequence of events seemed bound to derail the marriage. Nevertheless, the bride kept a genuine smile on her face and kept such a great outlook throughout the day. And the happily married couple just called me to shoot their newborn baby's first pictures, so all is well that ends well.

Sushi Centerpieces

- Nancy J. Taussig
Barefoot Weddings
www.barefootweddings.com

As the wedding officiant, I arrived early at a beachside wedding ceremony and reception venue. I noticed clear glass cylinders of water and rocks on the beautifully decorated dinner tables. I looked around and didn't see any boxes of flowers, so I asked if the florist was late. The onsite coordinator told me that goldfish were going into the cylinders very soon.

I don't know if it was chlorine in the water or if the water was too cold, but by the time the beach wedding ceremony was over and we walked back to the reception pavilion, all of the fish were dead!

The bridesmaids insisted that the groomsmen remove the "corpses" before the bride saw them. The groomsmen gallantly took off their jackets, rolled up their sleeves, and scooped out the dead fish, jokingly offering "sushi" to each other.

The tables ended up being decorated with cylinders of water and rocks — and the occasional dead fish the groomsmen didn't find. As I sat down in my chair, I realized there was still a dead goldfish at our table, but it was on my side of the cylinder and fortunately not on the side facing a little girl.

Most of the guests were unaware of the fish massacre, but I wonder how many of them thought cylinders full of water were strange centerpieces.

Bawling Bride

- Alison Decker

As a wedding caterer, I have seen faintings, boobs and more, but this wedding story takes the cake!

Let's call the bride Lisa and the groom Larry. Larry proposed to Lisa and they immediately began looking for wedding venues. They found the location they liked, only to discover they would have to wait over a year to get married there — there were no open Saturdays other than one in 3 months as a result of a cancellation. Instead of waiting, Lisa and Larry decided to take that Saturday spot and planned the whole wedding in a matter of weeks.

I met with Lisa and created a sit-down menu for 175 guests. We had several meetings hours in length discussing colors, flowers, pricing, etc. The days leading up to the wedding were a little hectic, and Lisa was stressed, but as weddings usually go, everyone showed up and the day began smoothly.

Then, for some reason still unknown to me, Lisa got very emotional prior to her ceremony and would not come out of the bridal room. Finally, the officiant went and banged on the door. The DJ had to play the Wedding March twice before Lisa finally walked down the aisle.

Once the ceremony concluded, the DJ began playing standard cocktail hour music. Now, the DJ had been hired literally the night before the wedding, so there was no order of events or any sort of playlist created. Unbeknownst to him, the song Lisa wanted for her First Dance was in his "wedding mix" that played during the cocktail hour. This sent Lisa into another panic, and she locked herself back in the bridal room and refused to come out.

Over an hour went by — guests were seated for dinner and waiting for their meals. Everyone was extremely intoxicated by this point and only getting worse without dinner. As the bride and groom had originally wanted, we served the salads as people were sitting down for the reception, until the Mother of the Bride started yelling, "No one eats before my baby!"

The groom finally appeared and encouraged the guests to begin dinner — without the bride. Everyone was relieved, except the wedding was so rushed that the couple didn't even have cards telling us what people were eating. We had to go up to each of 175 guests and ask them if they wanted beef or chicken! It took forever, and created huge chaos in the kitchen.

As we served dinner to all the guests, Lisa and Larry slipped in the door — no grand entrance, but the guests didn't notice. Lisa had obviously been crying and the groom was at a loss for what to do. To make matters worse, Lisa's parents and much of the bridal party were extremely upset with Lisa and making a huge uproar about it during the dinner hour.

Getting some food calmed Lisa down, enough to cut her cake and attempt to dance and have a good time. The wedding concluded promptly at 10 p.m., and I watched as Lisa stormed out of her reception. Larry said his goodbyes to his family and most people began filing slowly out of the hall.

We began tearing down everything and packing up dishes and linens. As I was finally walking out to my vehicle to head home, I heard a voice calling my name. I turned to find the bride, in her wedding dress, makeup running, tears and everything, asking if I could do her a favor. "Of course," I replied. Anything for the bride on her wedding day, right?

She wanted to know if I would be willing to take her home! I said of course and told her to get in. Then I snuck over to the owner of our catering business to let him know I was taking the bride home. (After the way this wedding went it wasn't as shocking to him as you might think.)

Lisa got in my car and we drove all the way to her hotel room, 20 minutes away. She was crying and very upset the whole time, telling me what a waste of money this was, how Larry was not the groom she thought he should be, and how her parents were wrong for being so mean to her. I asked her repeatedly if she wanted to call her husband or her parents and she refused. She said she just wanted to be left alone.

I dropped Lisa off at the hotel room she had stayed in the night before the wedding — her husband apparently had no idea where it was. She told me I was the best caterer ever because I took her home. She kept asking me if I agreed with and understood what she was saying about Larry and her family ... all I could say was, "Yes, definitely, I understand." I think that was my state of shock speaking!

The next day, everyone was naturally wondering what had happened. After the wedding, everyone had gone looking for Lisa to get into the limo they had rented, but, of course, she was nowhere to be found. Also, she had a very young daughter who was the flower girl at the wedding, whom she had left at the reception. The groom had been walking around with her daughter, looking for his bride! Luckily I had told that *one* person that she was with me and word had spread quickly about how the caterer had taken the bride home from her own wedding.

Post-wedding drama, we tried sending emails and satisfaction surveys to get some sort of idea what happened to Lisa and Larry afterwards, but with no response. We don't even know if they are still married. The officiant, venue coordinator, DJ and many other vendors agree with me that this was the craziest wedding any of us have ever seen!

Rain or Shine

- LuAnn Parks
Timeless Weddings of MS
www.timeless-weddings.net

I coordinated a wedding this past May where the wedding party itself consisted of 33 members, in addition to the bride and groom. The ceremony was held in a local church, and it was packed with friends and family, about 150 all together. The whole ceremony at the church went off without a hitch, and the wedding party was chauffeured to the reception site in not one, but two white stretch Hummers.

The reception was going to be held on the patio area of the local country club. Fourteen round dining tables, covered in sunset orange crush-satin cloths, were placed all around the country club pool, which featured floating lily pads and votive candles. The centerpieces on the tables were 18-inch-tall clear glass vases filled with bright orange, red, fuchsia, and yellow flowers with lush greenery. Calligraphy table numbers in frames were sitting on easels and a candid framed photo of the bride and groom was on each table. The place settings were in gold and crystal with gold chargers and red linen napkins. There were gold chairs with iridescent orange satin sashes. It was a lavish and beautiful landscape for a party.

The guests started arriving and the wedding party made their grand entrance after departing the Hummers in front of the country club. Things were just perfect ... pictures were being snapped by the photographer, the DJ was cranked up, beverages were being poured at the open bar, the buffet line was opened, and guests were laughing and hugging each other and starting to have a good time.

I was making the final check with the caterer when I heard this huge commotion outside. I spun around to look out the large window to the pool area, and I saw bridesmaids jumping up in the air, gold chargers flying, and food dropping into the pool! I went to the French doors and was run over by guests who were seeking shelter from this torrential downpour of rain that came from *nowhere*! As I pushed my way outside, the winds were gusting up to 60 miles an hour! My floral centerpieces and satin tablecloths were being blown down the hill to the 7th tee of the golf course. The DJ was running like a madman trying to get his electrical equipment under the shelter of the covered patio.

All 175-plus guests (the groom had been on the phone calling his buddies saying, "Yeah, come on out. The drinks and food are on us!"), the DJ and his equipment, the buffet tables, groom's cake and bride's cake tables, and the punch fountain all had to be squeezed into a little room that was only meant for the buffet line. Everyone who had been served before the rain started had to be re-served because a lot of the food ended up in the pool. The caterer was not happy at all. Also, there were only a few chairs for people to sit in and those were delegated to the elderly.

But soon enough, the bar was flowing again, the DJ cranked up the music even louder, and everyone was barefoot and soaked to the skin but enjoying themselves.

I checked the weather forecast on my Blackberry and was seeing hours more of this type of weather coming through our area. It rained like that, with gusting winds, for the next three hours! As the reception rocked on, I walked down the dark, slippery hill to the 7th tee, soaked to the skin, muddy and barefoot, collecting my floral arrangements and table cloths. I started folding the heavy, soaked table cloths, collecting flower vases and bridesmaids' bouquets, mirrors, and gold chargers, and placing them under the safety of the covered patio until I could sort it all out and start reloading my van.

But you know what? The bride and groom had the best time ever. I received so many compliments about the whole evening from guests and the bride's family who laughed throughout the hideous, soaked mess. The bride and groom were so thankful and happy as they were whisked off to their honeymoon by one of the Hummers. It was like no one even noticed the "little rainstorm" we had.

I never would have dreamed that wedding would have turned out that way — horribly wet and ruined, but yet still so memorable for so many people.

Fondant Fender Bender

- Caitlyn Fowler

My husband and I had our wedding reception at a beautiful, secluded ranch about 20 miles from the town where we got married. This meant that all our vendors had to drive through pretty narrow backroads to get to the location. It was June, and I guess we underestimated the amount of lake and mountain visitors who would be on the road that day. Between vacationers on their way in and out of town, as well as my own wedding traffic, the drive was pretty slow going.

As we sat in stop-and-go traffic, my mind was spinning: Would we have enough time for all the photos we were scheduled to take? Would the caterers be waiting on us to serve dinner? I completely forgot the fact that we had paid extra to have our baker hand-deliver our wedding cake herself.

Now, our cake was a detail I had slaved over. I dragged my husband to half a dozen cake tastings before choosing our baker. I really wanted the elegant look of fondant and pulled sugar to create a cake that looked like it was covered in lace. Just seeing the cake in person

was something I was really looking forward to.

I'm sure you know what comes next: In a rush to get the reception in all the traffic, the baker had to stop short, was rear-ended by another car, and the cake went crashing.

The whole time I was discussing our options my husband was shouting, "We like cookies and cream!"

As soon as she called, I knew something was wrong; she was practically in tears. I can only imagine how pathetic our beautiful four-tiered confection must have looked after the accident.

"Can you salvage it?" I asked, hoping that maybe even one layer could be saved. She just said, "No. I'm sorry."

I know it's silly, but I felt like one of our important guests had canceled! To make matters worse, my husband could have cared less. He joked, "Tell her to pick up an ice cream cake from the grocery store!" The whole time I was discussing our options with the baker, my lovely husband was shouting, "We like cookies and cream!" He thought it was hilarious; I was exasperated. The baker promised to figure something out, and I tried to enjoy my champagne and the rest of our limo ride to the reception.

Once we got to the ranch, after photos, I sent one of our groomsmen to check on a few things, such as the caterer and the baker. I was very curious to see what Plan B she had come up with — especially since we paid a pretty penny for our custom design. When the groomsman came back, he had a big smile and assured me, "It's fine, don't worry."

I have to admit, right after we made our grand entrance, I went to check things out. Thankfully, our baker came through. The small cake table had been replaced with a long table covered in an array of different desserts. The baker had immediately called her assistant, who rushed over to the wedding with anything and everything they had at their flagship store.

So, we didn't have our lace-inspired cake, but we did have fruit tarts, mini pies, fudge, gourmet cupcakes and more. Our guests who were unaware of the mishap commented later that our "dessert buffet" was fantastic and unexpected. I just laughed — definitely unexpected!

Baby on the Way

- Colleen Redding
Redding Photography
www.redding-photography.com

I was on my way to Palm Springs to photograph the wedding of a young couple where the bride-to-be was 7 months pregnant. Per her request, I called the Mother of the Bride to let her know that I was on my way and to discuss at what time the bride would be ready for her photographs. When she picked up the phone she informed me that they were on their way to the hospital, as the bride was having signs of labor. She told me not to worry she was sure they would make it to the wedding. I reassured her that everything would be fine and continued to the wedding location as planned.

I arrived at the location right on time, about two hours before the wedding was to take place. The Mother of the Bride and I kept in touch throughout this time. She tried to remain confident that her daughter would make it to her wedding. The wedding staff had everything prepared, the DJ was all set up, and eventually the guests started arriving.

After a short time, word got out to everyone that the bride was indeed in labor, 2 months early, and would not be making it to her wedding day. The family requested that everyone enjoy the reception as planned. Although the mother had phoned me and told me I could leave, I felt it was only right to stay and photograph the reception. After all, this family paid a lot of money to have the wedding and they should at least have photographs to show them what it was like. It was a touching reception with family and friends celebrating this couple and praying for them and their child.

A few hours into the reception a family member brought his laptop out and began a slideshow of photographs. The slideshow played photos of the couple and their closest family, Maid of Honor and Best Man in the hospital, where the minister

> They were on their way to the hospital, as the bride was having signs of labor.

married the couple right there in the delivery room. They were very touching photographs for everyone at the reception.

The doctors managed to hold off labor a little for this bride, and she ended up having her daughter the very next day, on Christmas Eve. Because her daughter was born prematurely she had to spend 2 months in the hospital. When the baby was healthy enough to leave the hospital I photographed their first family portrait session — a perfect end to their wedding memories, and the perfect start to the rest of their lives together.

Getting Your Sea Legs

- Danielle Arroyo

My fiancé and I knew we wanted to get married near the water. We had taken a San Diego harbor cruise that we really loved, so we thought, why not *on* the water?! For our small wedding, we decided to rent a boat to sail out into the harbor at sunset while guests enjoyed cocktails and dancing onboard. It was summer in San Diego, when the evenings are just beautiful and the sunsets are amazing, so we were very excited.

I suppose it crossed my mind that some people aren't boat people, but the wedding invitations described the evening perfectly, so I figured guests would plan ahead for things like weather … and seasickness.

All our guests boarded the boat around 5 p.m. and we held our ceremony while the boat was docked. About 45 minutes later, the boat started to sail out in the harbor and toward Coronado Bridge. It was a bit windy, but not too rocky, as the bar opened and guests started getting cocktails. We were chatting with some friends when the wedding coordinator came up to me and whispered that some people were not feeling well. I told her to bring them some seltzer water and continued greeting my guests.

I guess that wasn't a good solution, because by the time we were ready to be seated for dinner, there was a line of seasick guests gathering outside the boat's one bathroom! Distressed, I asked around for the wedding coordinator, who was no where to be found. It turns out she was sick also! It got so bad that the captain started handing out plastic trash bags for guests to vomit into! We were horrified.

My husband and I don't get seasick at all, so it never occurred to me to recommend or hand out something to prevent motion sickness. My oversight meant that dinner had to be postponed until we finally made the call to sail back and re-dock the boat.

With the boat docked, our reception wasn't as quiet or intimate as we planned (there were tons of tourists walking up and down the harbor walk, staring at us and even taking pictures all evening), although it was still a beautiful night. The stars were out and the city even shot off fireworks, which was unexpected and we really enjoyed. And everyone was much relieved to be back near dry land.

If suppose I learned the lesson that if you're going to be planning a unique wedding, such as a ceremony and reception in the forest, a beach or on a boat, you should remind guests to prepare for the elements, such as wearing warm clothing, bringing bug spray or sunscreen, or making sure they take Dramamine before they come.

Banquet Room Blackout

- Judy Lawson

I was married in a small, lovely chapel a bit out in the country, and the reception was 20 minutes away in a hotel banquet room. It was a sunny, cold but not freezing winter day. The wedding went beautifully, from my brother singing a solo to the bagpiper who marched in at the end of the ceremony to lead us back down the aisle.

On the way to the reception, we were coming up over a small hill heading toward the city of Ann Arbor, Michigan, when I noticed it seemed unusually dark. The stoplight ahead of us was out; as I looked around, I realized I couldn't see any lights at all. I started to breathe fast — there must have been a power outage! My brand-new husband said "Judy, don't panic, it's going to be OK."

As we drove into the parking lot of the hotel, I could see my brothers trying to direct cars and waving so people would know they were in the right place. We walked into the hotel and were greeted by a number of guests who all tried to be supportive. A hotel event manager approached us and said, "OK, we are working on getting the generator to work and we've called the electric company to request they make our area a priority for repairs. We've lit up the reception room with candles. It's really beautiful if you'd like to see it." Speechless, I followed her to the room, which indeed was aglow with candles everywhere. "Oh, this is really nice," I said, "I think we can make this work!"

The hotel event manager then said, "Well, there is only one problem. If the lights don't come on, we won't be able to serve your dinner — it would be against codes we have to follow." My heart sank. The guests were hungry, the food was ready, but we couldn't eat it?

> "Maybe we could order pizza?" someone said. I don't know who that was, but I wanted to smack them!

I walked back out to the lobby in the darkness. Suggestions started to fly. My boss said she could make a few calls and get us a space at the University of Michigan and we could order in some food. "Maybe we could order pizza?" someone said. I don't know who that was, but I wanted to smack them! Pizza?

I couldn't believe this was happening. My husband said it didn't matter what we ate or where we were. I knew he was right. We had all meandered into the banquet room lit with candles and were chatting and waiting. About 30 minutes had passed, when suddenly the lights came on!

Within 15 minutes, dinner was served, and the rest of the night was perfect.

I'm glad we didn't make any quick decisions and just held on for a while. And, in a way, having our reception almost ruined made us realize what was really important about our wedding day. And I still remember how beautiful the candlelit reception hall looked.

Nosedive

- Nayeli Cerpas

After my rehearsal dinner, the night before my wedding, I stayed up late to make sure we had everything ready for our Big Day, and to clean (I always clean when I'm nervous). I must have gone to bed between 1 and 2 a.m. In a fitful sleep, I jerked from one side of the bed to the other and bumped, nose first, into the wall.

The thump was so loud that my now-husband jumped out of bed and quickly turned on the lights to see what was wrong. Half asleep, I told him to come back to bed. He looked at me, horrified, and I soon realized I had blood dripping down my face. He ran to get an ice pack and had me hold it on my face for a couple of hours while I snoozed.

The next morning, luckily, I didn't have a swollen nose, but I did have a big scrape! The makeup artist (in his infinite wisdom), plastered tons of makeup on my nose on the fresh scrape, which worked for a few hours until I started scarring and it showed through. In a quick emergency plan, one of my bridesmaids put red lipstick on me (and more concealer) to divert attention from my nose.

With 300-plus guests, I was worried that everyone would only look at my nose. Luckily, I had the most amazing time at my wedding and nothing, not even if I had broken my nose, could have changed that. I danced the night away and, somehow, none of the pictures showed the scrape — thank goodness!

The scar is *still* not gone, but I laughed about the incident that day and we still do now.

Sandbags, Anyone?

- Cristin Mowrer

On our wedding day it started to rain right before we arrived to the church. The weather channels had been calling for scattered showers so everyone thought it would pass. It had been bright and sunny at my parents' house all morning! The ceremony went on, and the rain continued. We took photographs at the church with our families, and the rain continued.

After the ceremony, got in our limos to head to the country club, which was a quarter-mile away. The roads were flooding and water was splashing up everywhere as we drove. Our 5-minute, 1-turn drive became every bride's worst nightmare. The road that our reception was on was closed! We drove to the next block, turned left, then had to make a U-turn because that road was closed. We tried the next block — same thing. That's when we saw a large emergency vehicle driving past us with rescue rafts in tow!

At this point, my husband and I started to panic. What would happen if we could not get to the country club? What if our guests could not get to the country club? Our bridal party came to the rescue. They began to call other guests who had gone back to the hotel in between and instructed them that the roads were closed. They rerouted the shuttle bus driver as well. One of our groomsmen grew up in that same neighborhood and helped our limo drive navigate his way to the reception. One hour later, we arrived at our country club to see 2 feet of standing water in the parking lot. The front door was inaccessible because of the water. There were trees falling down in the field across the street because the ground was so saturated.

That's when we saw a large emergency vehicle driving past us with rescue rafts in tow!

The limo drivers worked with the country club manager to get us in through the kitchen door. They laid out table cloths on the ground to cover the mud and the drivers took each of us in one at a time under multiple huge umbrellas! We all got inside without getting wet. Our drivers were fantastic.

We were still panicked that the guests would have trouble arriving, but the staff at the country club managed to solve the drainage issues after we arrived but before the guests did. Turns out there were 5 inches of rain that afternoon in a 1-hour window!

We ended up having an incredible party that we extended for an extra hour. Everyone I have spoken with has told us it was one of the nicest weddings they have ever been to. No one even cared about the flooding! And every single guest made it.

The only drawback was that we lost a lot of our time for pictures so we have very few pictures — only about 3 different ones — of my husband and I alone on our wedding day. However, we are getting dressed up again and heading back to the site for a photo session just the two of us. We certainly had a day no one will ever forget, and I get to wear my dress again.

Honeymoon

Honeymoon Registry Hoopla

- Carly Palmer-Benson

Two years ago my husband and I had a real oh-my-god-I-can't-believe-this wedding moment. We were invited to the wedding of an old sorority sister of mine. I hadn't seen her in a few years but was excited that we'd get to spend time with her and some old friends, since my husband and I went to the same college.

My friend and her fiancé were planning a big Southern wedding on the beach in Charleston, South Carolina. In lieu of gifts, they created a honeymoon registry to pay for their gorgeous honeymoon in St. Lucia. They asked for contributions for everything from a private villa to couple's massages on the beach. My husband and I ended up spending $150 on a snorkeling tour from their registry. To be honest, I was jealous!

As the months went by, my husband and I booked our plane tickets to Charleston, our beachfront bed and breakfast, and began making plans to see our friends who were also invited. Then, about two months before the wedding, I got an email from a friend who asked if I'd heard the news — the wedding had been called off!

Honeymoon Registry Hoopla

The groom had been caught cheating with a coworker and our friend had canceled the wedding. I certainly felt awful for her. I left her a message giving my condolences and went to work canceling our reservations.

Unfortunately, my husband and I were stuck with two nonrefundable plane tickets. After much haggling with the airline, we were able to change the date of our flights with only a $100 penalty fee. That's when my husband brought up the honeymoon registry. I assured him my friend would cancel the registry and refund everyone's cash gifts, as anyone would expect.

However, no word came from the bride about the registry. I got in touch with another guest and learned that the bride had gone ahead and accepted the check from her registry! Apparently, her attitude was that she was a scorned woman and deserved a luxurious tropical vacation — on all of us!

I was fuming; I debated calling my friend and giving her a piece of my mind but finally decided against it. She had been through a lot, and I imagined she and her family were also out some money from the cancelled wedding. I'll admit I'm still pretty ticked off at her, though.

I recently saw her Facebook page and she is in a new, serious relationship. I'm going to seriously think twice about going to her next wedding!

Hospital Room Honeymoon

- Aubrey Baadsgaard Poffenberger

Kyle and I met at a mutual friend's birthday party in Philadelphia. We were immediately drawn to each other after our first introduction. Kyle saw me through the final stages of writing my dissertation and I helped him through the first years of medical residency. We both felt a deep, true, and tender love for each other and decided to marry on Valentine's Day 2009.

On the morning of the wedding, I felt weak and had some stomach pains but shrugged it off as the flu and happily made my way to the temple anticipating my Big Day. Upon entering the temple for the wedding ceremony, however, my stomach pains intensified and I found myself too weak to stand. I laid down on a couch, moaning and crying out in pain. Kyle sat at my side unsure of what to do. I finally gathered my courage and attempted to walk to the marriage room, when I was overcome with pain and nausea and had to be escorted to the nearest bathroom, where I began vomiting.

Unable to stand, I was placed in a wheelchair and, during a brief lapse in the pain, was wheeled, with vomit bag in hand, to the marriage altar. As I gazed into Kyle's eyes in midst of the pain I was suffering, tears streaming down my face, I felt intense feelings of love for him, and I could sense the same in his eyes.

Immediately after the ceremony, paramedics rushed me to the nearest hospital, where a CT scanned confirmed that I had acute appendicitis, and my appendix had probably already burst. I was rushed to emergency surgery about an hour later. My appendix had indeed ruptured and the infection covered all of my internal organs. The doctor performed laproscopic surgery to remove the appendix and used ten liters of water to wash out the infection.

After waking from surgery, I was brought to a recovery room, where Kyle was awaiting my arrival. The nurses put us in a quiet, secluded corner of the hospital so we could have some privacy and brought in a bed for Kyle so he could at least hold my hand on our wedding night. Kyle quietly reassured me that all would be alright, and we talked for a while about how to cancel our honeymoon, before I drifted off to sleep.

> I was placed in a wheelchair and wheeled, with vomit bag in hand, to the marriage altar.

Needless to say, we were the talk of the hospital. I was the infamous bride whose appendix burst on her wedding day. What are the odds? The nurses all tried to lessen my disappointment, kindly putting a sign reading "The Honeymoon Suite" with a gold bow and two red hearts on my hospital door.

The next day was particularly rough for both of us. We both cried together wondering how we were going to make it through our first few days together. Gone was the marriage of our dreams, the beautiful reception with bright red roses and purple lilies and a red velvet drape for our backdrop. Gone was our carefully planned dream honeymoon in exotic Spain. Instead, I was sick in a hospital bed, barely able to move and completely depressed. All of our waiting and planning had led simply to this hospital room, the very place Kyle was trying to escape for his wedding vacation (Kyle is a doctor and had been anticipating some time away from the hospital for the wedding).

After letting all my disappointment well up into an overflowing stream that spilled out of my heart and poured from my eyes, a feeling of peace at once overwhelmed me. It may not have been the wedding of my dreams, but it was still my wedding.

So, I decided to embrace our experience. It was sweet and tender beyond any that has yet come my way. I had found and married the man of my dreams and been saved from potential death (I could have been on a plane or in Spain when my appendix ruptured). My husband had been at my side all the way, healing, nourishing, and comforting me, carrying me when I had no strength, reaching out his hand and helping me move forward. I know that the depth of my love for my husband has increased one hundred-fold from my wedding-day disaster, and I wouldn't have it any other way.

Man Overboard?

- Kelly McBride-Schnure

How about losing your husband on the first night of your honeymoon on a cruise ship? I've been on 23 cruises, but this was my husband Rob's first. Once aboard the ship, we hit several of the bars. At 5:30 p.m., I left him at the pool bar to go unpack and get ready for dinner. He told me he would see me in the cabin at 7 p.m. to take a shower and go for a pre-dinner drink. But there was no Rob at 7, 7:15 or 7:30, so I told our cabin steward to let Rob know I went to dinner. I sat through dinner, by myself, at a table for two, on the first night of our honeymoon. I ate anyway, although I was furious.

I left the dining room and went searching at approximately 9:15. The bartenders at the pool bar were closing up and said, "Mister Rob was just here." There were still seven other bars he could have been in. I went to the Purser (the ship's head of accounting) to see what bar his ship card had last logged in a purchase — the pool bar! Thinking I had just missed him, I went to our cabin. No Rob, but there was evidence that he had taken a shower and changed.

I went back to the Purser and got a map of the bars and, one by one, I trekked through the entire ship looking for him, making another stop at the cabin halfway through to see if he was there — but still no Rob.

It was closing in on 11 p.m. Panicked, I called his mom from my cell phone (don't even ask me why, I didn't know where else to turn), all the time thinking the unthinkable — that he had fallen overboard. At that point, the Purser was actually worried and called security. They pulled up his ship card photo to see what he looked like. The Purser decided, even though it was very late, to do an "all-call" throughout the ship. An all-call actually shuts down any music throughout the ship and is the only call that can be heard inside the cabins, waking people up who were already asleep! The all-call was made ... still nothing.

> Panicked, I called his mom, all the time thinking the unthinkable — that he had fallen overboard.

Security went back down to the cabin, and he was still not there. We continued to make a round-robin of the bars to make sure we were not just missing him, but no Rob. A second all-call was made — by that time it was 12:30 in the morning, and I was quite sure that if any of the people we were waking up were to meet Rob, they would personally throw him overboard.

MAN OVERBOARD?

I was obviously upset, my mother-in-law kept calling, and security was buzzing everywhere. The Purser herself was getting very upset, and she suggested that she and I go to my cabin to wait there. Upon entering the cabin, I noticed the drapes billowing out slightly, which would mean the sliding glass door was open. Sure enough, out on the balcony, in his underwear, iPod headphones on and dancing, was my darling husband. The Purser and I both hugged him as he was asking, "What, what's the matter?" We both proceeded to give him what was due.

The next day, Rob stayed by my side. All the crew members knew who he was, and the Purser even joked that there were leashes for sale in the gift shop. Rob was very red and very quiet but good-natured about the whole thing. Crew members were constantly saying, "Hi Rob — get lost anywhere recently?" Needless to say, he did not live this down during the entire 10-day cruise.

Honeymoon Mugging

- Amanda and Paul Jameson

My husband and I planned a two-week-long honeymoon that started in Florence, Italy and let us tour several other Italian cities, including Rome, Venice, and the Italian Riviera. Neither of us had ever been to Europe, and we were very excited.

On our second day in Florence, the weather was sunny and beautiful, so we decided to stop by a few of the shops along our street and make a picnic lunch. We bought fruit, cheese, meat, and a bottle of Chianti and went to a nice public park. We were really enjoying ourselves when a man walked up, squatted down and started talking to us. He was asking us questions in English about our vacation when another man suddenly appeared behind Paul, my husband. I started to get very nervous, and sure enough, the second man pulled out a knife! The first man told us in English that we shouldn't yell or act differently and to give him our watches, cash, camera and wedding rings! Paul started to hesitate, but I was so scared, I told him, "Just give him everything."

After a minute, the men were gone. Paul and I just looked at each other in shock and disbelief. I burst into tears; our day was ruined and our wedding rings, which we'd only had for a few days, were gone. We went back to our hotel and drank the bottle of wine, feeling fairly miserable. Paul had to call our insurance company about the stolen rings and other belongings. I just kept saying, "I can't believe we got mugged on our honeymoon!"

Luckily, we still had our passports, which we'd left in the hotel safe that day. The next day we took the train to Rome where we were excited to be staying in a quaint villa-hotel we'd read about in several travel articles. The hotel was family run and we were looking forward to the homemade breakfast served each morning in the garden. However, we were in for quite a surprise when we got there!

We couldn't prove we were married!

When we went to put our luggage in our room, we found it had twin beds — not what we'd requested, obviously. Paul went down to ask to be moved and the man at the front desk told him they only give double beds to married couples. When Paul explained that we were married, the man gestured to Paul's ring finger, pointing out that he wasn't wearing a wedding ring. The absence of rings, plus the fact that our passports had different names on them, meant we couldn't prove we were married. At that point we were so exhausted from traveling and arguing that we said, "Forget it," and simply pushed the twin beds together for an uncomfortable night of sleep.

Needless to say, this didn't start our honeymoon off on a very good note. Thankfully, we did enjoy our time in other cities, especially the beach cities of the Italian Riviera. Paul learned how to say, "Our wedding rings were stolen" in Italian, too. We thought, all's well that ends well — until we went to fly back to Paris to fly home.

I am terrified of flying. I spent the first hour of our flight to Europe clutching Paul's arm until it practically turned blue. Every single bump and thump on the plane nearly brings me to tears. When we checked in for our flight, the airline we'd booked on put Paul and I in different rows, not next to each other. They refused to switch us so we could sit together. I started panicking, telling Paul I wouldn't get on the plane. The more he told me to calm down, the more hysterical I got. I yelled at the woman at the airline counter that I hated Europe, that everyone was rude, and I was never coming back. A crazy American, I know.

Thankfully, Paul was able to fight through the language barrier to get someone to switch seats with him. I was honestly just so glad to be going home.

Although our honeymoon didn't end up being the stress-free vacation we'd imagined, we did have some romantic and fun memories, and we certainly have a crazy story to tell at parties.

No Shoes,
No Service

- Pam Sherman

My husband and I planned an amazingly romantic honeymoon to Bora Bora. He was very excited about the special reservations he made for our last night on the island, at Villa Moana, which is one of the nicest restaurants in Bora Bora. There is one table on its own level that they supposedly only give to honeymooners, and you have to book it far in advance.

I bought a new dress especially for this dinner. When the night arrived, I pulled out my nice jewelry, took extra time with my hair and makeup and was very excited for what was sure to be an elegant evening. We boarded the water taxi (one drawback to being in a deserted bungalow environment is it's very far away from everything!) and headed to dinner.

Each night, when we boarded the water taxi I would take off my shoes so my heels didn't get stuck in the cracks on the dock. When we got off the ferry I asked my husband to please hand me my shoes, only he didn't have them — he thought I did!

We watched the taxi speed off into the night, and there I was, dressed up for dinner without any shoes! The cab driver who was taking us to dinner called ahead, and the restaurant said they wouldn't let us in without shoes on. Thinking fast, the driver gave me his (huge, smelly, sweaty!) loafers to borrow!

If I weren't on my honeymoon I would probably have been mortified, but it was too funny not to laugh and just go with it!

Ski-Lift Snafu

- Roseanne and Clark Furr

Clark and I are ski buffs, so we planned a beautiful honeymoon in the Swiss Alps that actually coincided with my birthday. We couldn't wait to celebrate.

When we got to Zermatt we checked into our hotel and made plans for the week. I was really looking forward to skiing the Matterhorn, which is the famous peak between the borders of Switzerland and Italy. You can actually take the lift and ski down to the town of Cervinia, which is on the Italian side of the mountain. The next day was my birthday, so we planned to ski all day, then meet back up at the lodge for a drink before we went to a nice dinner for my birthday.

That next day, my husband and I had a lovely traditional Swiss breakfast and went out to the lifts. We skied together for a while, then stopped for lunch. After lunch, my husband mentioned that he wanted to try some extra-challenging runs, so we decided to go our separate ways. We agreed to meet back at 4 p.m. to have time for a drink and a hot shower before our dinner reservations.

After a while on my own, I thought I might like to ski down the Italian side of the mountain. What I didn't realize was that the Italian side is an extremely long run and the lift-link back to the Swiss side closes at 3 p.m. When I got to the bottom, I snapped a few photos of the mountain and went to get back on the lift — which I then learned had closed for the day.

> I asked how long it would take to get back. The cab driver replied, "Maybe 5 hours. Maybe."

I didn't panic at first. I thought, *This must happen all the time; there must be a bus or train of some sort.* I started asking around. No bus and no train, I was told. I thought, *That's ridiculous. These people must not understand what I'm asking.* But many people spoke perfect English, and I soon started to worry that I'd made a big mistake. I got out my cell phone and called our hotel and asked them the best way to get back to the Swiss side of the mountain. The concierge told me to find a taxi cab, but I could hear the concern in his voice.

I trudged off in my ski boots to find a taxi. Finally, I did and I explained I needed to go back to Zermatt. I asked how long it would take, as I was expected to meet my husband shortly. The cab driver replied, "Maybe 5 hours." Five hours! "Maybe," he reinforced. "How much?" I asked, now starting to panic. He quoted what would have been more than $250. I stared at him blankly.

Backing away from the taxi, I called my husband and explained the situation. "Two-hundred and fifty dollars?" he repeated. He checked with the hotel and confirmed this was the reality. I was stuck on the Italian side of the mountain, alone, in soaking wet clothes, on my birthday.

I started to sob on the phone. I was freezing and tired and was missing out on spending time with my husband — on our honeymoon! Ever the calm one, my husband assured me we would be fine and to go get a hotel for the night.

So, I spent my birthday, the first real night of our honeymoon, shivering in a hotel bed, wrapped in the hotel's bathrobe while my sopping wet ski clothes attempted to dry. I ordered room service, including a glass of wine and a big mug of hot tea, and fell asleep after a good cry. I will admit I was feeling pretty sorry for myself. You better believe I was in the front of the lift-link line first thing the next morning.

When I finally found Clark he hugged me for what seemed like 5 minutes! And he didn't leave my side the rest of our honeymoon.

The funniest part was, on the plane ride home, we finally pulled out the guidebook we'd brought but never opened. And right there, in bold letters, was a warning not to miss the last lift back when skiing in Zermatt!

Skip the Lobster Salad

- Kristie Koehn

Due to our schedules, my new husband and I weren't allotted much time for a honeymoon. We decided to enjoy a three-day weekend at a local luxury hotel.

Our suite was beautiful, the views magnificent and my parents were footing the bill — what more could we ask for? The hotel featured two restaurants and on our second night we decided to try out one of them. My husband dined on steak, while I decided to be adventurous and order the Maine Lobster Salad.

All was well until later in the evening my stomach started to rumble fiercely. We got back to our room and once 10 o'clock hit, it was on — food poisoning! I don't think that suite's toilet ever saw such attention from any individual's top and bottom half! Every 15 minutes this continued up until 6 a.m.

At that point, we thought it best to get me to the hospital as I was so weak and dehydrated. We drove to the closest hospital, which was not in the best end of town, thus I was frisked and put through a metal detector before I could be seen by a doctor.

The hospital staff hooked me up with an IV valve in order to host a plethora of medication and fluids. However, it wasn't set up correctly, so when the needle hit my vein blood sprayed everywhere! By then, I looked like a pale, emaciated Carrie. Needless to say, my honeymoon was not sweet as honey.

Conclusion

Send us your crazy, funny or outrageous true wedding stories for a future edition of this book or any of our other wedding planners. If you would like to submit your story for consideration, please email info@WSPublishingGroup.com and put "OMG Wedding Stories" in the subject line. Or, write to us at WS Publishing Group, 7290 Navajo Road, Suite 207; San Diego, California 92119.

If your story is selected, we will contact you with the good news!

Please make your engagement, wedding or honeymoon story 300 words or more and include the following information:

This is to authorize WS Publishing Group to use our story in any of their upcoming books. WS Publishing Group (can), (cannot) use our name when telling our story. I also (am), (am not) interested in participating in a radio/TV interview tour.

Your name:
Your signature:
Spouse's name (if applicable):
Spouse's signature:
Your wedding business (if applicable):
Your Website (if applicable):
Phone number:
E-mail:

Thank you for reading *OMG! Wedding Stories From WedSpace.com*. We hope you enjoyed our WedSpace.com members' crazy but true wedding tales!

WeddingSolutions.com

Everything You Need to Plan Your Dream Wedding

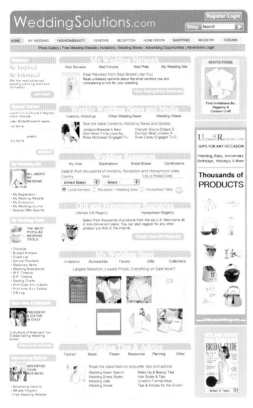

- The Latest Wedding Gowns
- Comprehensive Wedding Planning Tools
- Articles, Tips & Advice
- Thousands of Local Vendors
- Beautiful Reception Sites
- Honeymoon Destinations
- Largest Online Wedding Store
- Wedding Forums
- Personal Wedding Website
- Honeymoon & Gift Registry
- Polls, News, Videos, Media
- Wedding Planning Certification Programs

SEARCH FOR WEDDING GOWNS

View the Latest Designs

Search for your perfect wedding gown by designer, style and price.

SEARCH FOR RESOURCES

Reputable & Reliable

Find local vendors, reception, honeymoon & destination wedding sites.

Log on to www.WeddingSolutions.com for more information

WeddingSolutions.com

FREE Wedding Website on WeddingSolutions.com

$99 Value

Includes 19 Custom Pages

- Home
- Our Story
- Photo Gallery
- Details of Events
- Wedding Party
- Registry
- Local Info
- City Guide
- Accommodations
- Things to Do

- Restaurants
- Guest Book
- View Guest Book
- Sign Guest Book
- Wedding Journal
- Honeymoon
- Miscellaneous
- RSVP
- Contact Us
- Much More

SAVE UP TO $200 ON WEDDING INVITATIONS & ACCESSORIES

Invitations . . . .

SAVE up to $100

- Wedding Invitations
- Engagement
- Bridal Shower
- Rehearsal Dinner
- Casual Wedding
- Seal 'n Send
- Save The Date
- Direction Cards
- Programs
- Thank-You Notes
- Much More!

Accessories . . . .

SAVE up to $100

- Toasting Glasses
- Attendants' Gifts
- Unity Candles
- Aisle Runners
- Cake Tops
- Flower Girl Basket
- Ring Pillow
- Guest Book
- Cake Knife & Server
- Favors
- Much More!

Log on to www.WeddingSolutions.com/specialoffers
for more details on these offers

- Gifts from the top U.S. merchants

- Compare products and prices

- Simplified notification process saves you time

- Same Merchants, Same Products, 1 Registry!

Already have everything you need or want?

Help those in need through our Charity Registry

Request that your guests donate much needed products to the charity of your choice in lieu of wedding gifts.

"Give a Gift" allows your guests to donate much needed products to the charity of your choice.

Your guests will be able to select from hundreds of national and local charities and see their "wish list" of the items they need most such as blankets, office supplies and more.

Your guests can then purchase these products in your name and they will be sent directly to the charity of your choice.